The Ultimate Indian Cookbook

Meera Budhwar

Quantum
Books

A QUANTUM BOOK

This book is produced by
Quantum Publishing
6 Blundell Street
London N7 9BH

ISBN 978-1-84573-467-1

QUMTUIND

Digitised by Quadrum Solutions, Mumbai, Indian
www.quadrumltd.com

Cover design by Dave Jones, www.euro-designs.info

Consultant Editors: Meera Budhwar and Caroline Smith
Managing Editor: Julie Brooke
Project Editor: Samantha Warrington
Assistant Editor: Jo Morley
Production Manager: Rohana Yusof
Publisher: Sarah Bloxham

Printed in Singapore by
Star Standard Industries Pte Ltd
The material in this publication previously appeared in *Complete Indian Cookbook*,
Indian Regional Cooking, *Step-by-Step Indian Cooking* and *Indian Vegetarian Cooking*.

Contents

Introduction

India is a land of spectacular contrasts, from the emerald Vale of Kashmir in the snow-clad mountains of the north to the steaming jungles and palm-fringed beaches of the tropical south. Across this vast country of more than a billion inhabitants the intricate use of spices unites all the kitchens of the land in producing food that is uniquely Indian.

There are about 25 spices on the shelf in the Indian pantry. Many of them will have come from the back garden along with fresh herbs and bulbs – onions, garlic and shallots. With this huge treasury of flavours the Indian cook can create an infinite number of different dishes. Spices can be used individually or combined, roasted or ground with water into a paste to produce flavours anywhere on the spectrum from sweet to sour, fiery to bland and fragrant to pungent.

Indians are almost intuitively aware of the medicinal properties of the herbs and spices they use to flavour their food, and they eat not just for sheer enjoyment and to stay alive, but to keep their bodies healthy and well-tuned. Apart from their medicinal properties, spices and other condiments can be used to offset the extremes of temperature. In the north, warming spices take the bite out of freezing winter days, and in the south bittersweet tamarind has a soothing effect in the airless midday heat.

Of course what is eaten also depends largely on local produce. Broadly speaking, bread is eaten in the north and rice in the south. In the south the food tends to be more fiery (and paradoxically more refreshing, even if it does bring tears to the eyes). In Kerala, in particular, grow the coconut palms, the tamarind and jackfruit trees and the spice gardens that made Cochin rich and famous.

In the south, the tropical heat is put to use to mature pickles and for overnight fermentation of bread and cakes made from ground peas without the addition of yeast. Southerners often steam their food, whereas in the north it is oven cooked. In Rajasthan in the northwest, picnickers make an impromptu oven by digging a pit for a cow-dung fire on which they will cook spiced meat in a clay pot. The lid of the pot is sealed with dough, and more burning dung is heaped over it. This technique is called *dum*– food is baked slowly all the way through and all the juices are kept in, resulting in the tenderest meat and the richest possible flavour.

In Kashmir the winters are made bearable by cooking with warming spices, particularly cinnamon. People carry around baskets of live charcoal to keep the cold at bay between meals, and these baskets serve a double purpose, often baking an egg or a potato for a hot snack.

Kashmir is a land of lakes and tranquil water gardens. The lakes produce abundant fish and delicious lotus roots. Ingenious farmers make floating vegetable gardens from reeds and mud, which can be towed about or left to drift picturesquely at anchor. When they are harvested, vegetables are sold from boats at the floating market. As autumn draws in there is a frenzy of mushroom picking and all kinds of vegetables, especially chillies, are hung up on the rafters to dry to keep the family supplied when the snows come. To see them through the winter, the Kashmiris make a dried spice cake called *ver*, crushing their spices according to a family recipe, then mixing them to a paste with mustard oil. The cake is hung up and bits are broken off it as required.

In the east, the Bengalis are noted for their love of fish and their insatiable desire for sweets, especially jaggery (raw sugar). Sugar cane is pressed to extract the juice, which is then heated over wood fires and patiently stirred for many hours until it is thick enough to set. Lumps of it are eaten as sweets and the Bengalis are so fond of it that they even manage to slip it into their vegetable curries.

Bombay in Maharashtra on the west coast, India's Hollywood and boom town founded on seven islands, has its own sweet treats – savoury scones made of rice flour. They take several days and many processes to make, and are served at religious festivals.

Lucknow in Uttar Pradesh glories in whole chickens stuffed with quails, and a celebration halva made from the yolks of 100 eggs. Another local extravagance is a pearl pilaf – a dish of rice and "pearls" made by stuffing a chicken's oesophagus with a mixture of egg yolks and real gold and silver, and tying it at intervals to resemble a string of pearls. It is then boiled and slit open, and the "pearls" pop out, looking very like the real thing.

All over India, the laws of religion rule what is eaten. Hindus are vegetarian, although the priestly caste of Kashmiri Brahmins do eat meat, abstaining instead from cooking with garlic and onions, which they believe inflame the passions. Jains are such strict vegetarians that they will neither eat root vegetables, for fear of killing insects as they dig, nor will they touch tomatoes or aubergines, whose colour reminds them of blood. The Muslims will not eat pork and nowhere except in the state of Kerala is it permitted to kill the sacred cow. One sect of Muslims, the Bohris, alternate salt and sweet dishes and begin their meal by eating a pinch of salt in praise of Allah.

Presenting the meal

The traditional way to serve Indian food is on a *thali* or large tray, often of beautiful wrought metal. Each different dish will be in a small metal or earthenware bowl perched around the edge of the tray, or laid out on a low communal brass table. The diners sit on the floor, or on very low stools. The carpet is spread with

Below left: From the exuberance of the Palace of the Four Winds at Jaipur to the simplicity of the local post office, India is a subcontinent with many architectural delights.

Below right: For most of the time the elephant is a humble beast of burden, earning its keep by carrying and pulling heavy loads, but on festive occasions it is profusely decorated and becomes the centre of much attention.

coloured cloth to protect it and the guests are given giant coloured napkins. The dishes can be wrapped in cotton or silk, which is loosely folded back over the food after it has been served. Often banana leaves will serve as disposable plates. More people today are sitting up to a table with chairs, although in many parts the men are still served first, and then the women eat together on the floor in the kitchen.

Indians eat with their hands. The right hand only is used – the left is thought unclean. In some parts of India the whole hand is used; in others just the fingertips. Generally, food is scooped up with a piece of flat bread in the north and mopped up with rice in the south. It means that cleanliness is very important – hands are washed before and after eating and water for washing is provided even on barrows selling snacks in the streets.

In all parts of India hospitality is legendary. All the dishes, including fruit and sweetmeats, are offered at once. Decoration is simple (nuts, chopped herbs, lemon slices) and sometimes exotic – silver and gold-leaf *vark* on special occasions provides a direct, although expensive, source of minerals.

Cold water is drunk with meals. Breakfast, which might be a sweet flaky bread in the foothills of the Himalayas, a potato curry in the capital, Delhi, or a steamed bean cake (*idli*) in the south, is served with tea, sometimes spiced with cinnamon, or with hot strong coffee. During the day an Indian might drink freshly pressed fruit juice (mango is the favourite), coconut milk (in the south), or lassi, a sweet or sometimes salty drink made from yoghurt. Muslims are forbidden alcohol, but there is plenty of potent liquor about for whose who want it. Other drinks include *asha*, which is distilled from jaggery, palm toddy and, of course, gin.

After a meal the hostess may offer betel leaves – glossy green leaves with mildly anaesthetic properties and a refreshing taste. These are chewed and then spat out (or more delicately removed), like gum. They can be taken neat or wrapped around nuts, quicklime, cardamom pods, cloves or tobacco. Shah Jahan, one of Indian's more colourful rulers and the builder of the Taj Mahal as a mausoleum for his wife Mumtaz, was even known to wrap them around poison for his less-welcome guests.

This book offers enticing meat dishes from the north; from the east, characteristic fish delicacies. The vegetable dishes originate mainly in the south and west. From the south, too, come coconut, hot spicy vegetable dishes and pulses. This is a comprehensive collection of recipes: the flavour is wholly Indian.

Spices and aromatics in the Indian kitchen

Spices and aromatics are the very heart of Indian cookery. Flowers, leaves, roots, bark, seeds and bulbs (the simplest of natural ingredients) are used in endless combinations to produce an infinite variety of flavours: sweet, sharp, hot, sour, spicy, aromatic, tart, mild, fragrant or pungent.

The Indian cook aims to create blends of spices so subtle that a completely new taste arises– something indefinable. Sometimes the flavour of one particular spice can be magnified by the careful underplay of several others. As many as 15 spices may be used in one dish, or there might be only one. Spices, unlike herbs, can be used together without loss of flavour.

It is best to buy your spices whole and to grind them at home (see page 20) if the recipe calls for it. Whole spices keep longer than spice powders, which quickly lose their aroma. But even whole spices begin to taste tired after a whilst so buy small quantities and keep them in airtight jars in a cool dark place. Do not buy curry powder – this is a blanket term for a blend of inferior spices which will make everything taste the same.

Asafoetida (Hing)
This is a resin and comes from Kashmir. It is bought ground and is said to smell of truffles. The flavour is quite pungent, but it is used mainly for its digestive properties, especially in the cooking of beans, where it combats flatulence. A pinch of it can be fried in hot oil before the rest of the ingredients are cooked.

Biriyani masala
This is a special sweet spice mix for biriyani dishes. Grind together the cardamom seeds from 8 pods, 25 g (1 oz) cinnamon stick, 6 cloves and 1 tsp fennel seeds.

Cardamom (Elaichi)
Pale green cardamom pods contain tiny black seeds and grow in the rainforests of southern India. They have a sweet fragrant flavour and can be used whole (although the pod is not usually eaten) or the seeds can be taken out of the pods and used separately. This is a fiddly business, but seeds are not usually sold out of their pods as they lose their flavour too

fast. Some recipes use ground cardamom seeds and as they are so small, it is best to grind them with a pestle and mortar.

Cayenne pepper (Pisi hui lal mirch)
Cayenne pepper, like paprika, comes from the seeds of plants in the capsicum family. It is a blend of various types of chilli powder. The capsicum family is large, ranging from the sweet pepper to the chilli. In general, the smaller the fruit, the hotter it is. Cayenne is sold as a powder. It should not be as hot as chilli powder, but it is pretty hot and should therefore be used with care.

Chilli (Mirchi)
Chilli is the hottest flavour on earth. Chillies and chilli powder should be used with extreme care. Do not take a bite of a chilli or even lick one to see how it tastes as the effect will be quite devastating. Also, do not touch your mouth or eyes while handling chillies – the burning will be intense. Whole chillies can be seeded to make them a little less hot. Regulate the quantity of chilli recommended in the recipes according to how much you can bear, and do not forget to tell your guests if you have left a whole chilli lurking in the curry.

You can now buy fresh chillies at many grocery shops and supermarkets. If you live a long way from a regular supplier of chillies, buy them when you see them, wash them, dry them, put them in a jar and fill it to the brim with oil. Screw the lid on tightly and keep them in a cool dark place. This is a very good way of storing them, and you get a flavoured oil out of it too. Otherwise chillies go mouldy quite quickly. If one is mouldy, all the others will be infected too and the whole lot should be thrown away.

Chillies go red as they ripen, so dried chillies are always red. They are dropped into hot oil to release their aroma before other ingredients are added.

Chilli powder is very hot indeed as it is made from the crushed seeds of the chilli, its hottest part. A blend of chilli, garlic, cumin and oregano is sometimes also sold as chilli powder.

Cinnamon (Dalchini)

Cinnamon has a rich, warm flavour. It is available as a powder but is much better bought in sticks. You can then break off a piece and add it to the curry. It should be discarded before serving. A lot of cinnamon is grown in Sri Lanka and it is the inner bark of a tree related to the laurel. The outer bark is scraped off and the inner bark peeled off in strips and rolled into sticks, which are then dried.

Cloves (Luong)

Cloves are the flower buds of an evergreen of the myrtle family. They have been used in India for thousands of years, not only in cookery, but to sweeten the breath and to relieve the pain of toothache. They contain a mild anaesthetic. Cloves are best bought whole and ground, if necessary, at home with a pestle and mortar. Whole cloves are not eaten, but left on the side of the plate.

Coconut (Narial)

Fresh coconut may be grated and frozen. You can buy desiccated coconut in packets in Indian shops or supermarkets, and this can be used if the fresh variety is not available. (For how to prepare coconut, see page 18.)

Coriander (Dhaniya)

The English name for this spice comes for the Greek *koros*, meaning 'bug'. They are small ridged seeds, light brown in colour, and can be easily squashed under the thumb. They are used powdered or whole.

Fresh green coriander (Hari)

The leaves of the coriander plant are rather like those of flat-leaf parsley, but darker and more brilliant. Fresh coriander can be quite expensive to buy, but it is just as easily grown as parsley and can be used in the same way, in English as well as Indian dishes. The leaves have a very distinctive bittersweet taste. The best way of keeping this herb is in a jug of water in the fridge. Tired leaves can be revived by immersing in cold water for an hour, but do not keep them in water as they will go slimy.

Cumin (Jeera)

Cumin seeds are long and slim, similar to caraway seeds, but have a distinctive warm aroma. They are used either whole or ground, and can be bought ground. However, it is best to buy them whole and grind your own at home, as the ground spice loses its flavour quite quickly. Cumin is often used roasted. Drop the whole seeds into a hot dry saucepan and cook until the roasted fragrance emerges. Shake the saucepan to prevent sticking. The seeds can be stored whole, or ground in a coffee grinder and stored or used immediately.

Curry leaves (Kari pulia or Neem)

These are small grey-greenish leaves, a bit like bay, and are grown in many Indian gardens. They can be used fresh or dried; the dried ones can be crumbled onto food, and their aroma is released by its heat and moisture. They are sometimes fried in the oil the food is cooked in, and then discarded. They can also be eaten.

Food colourings

Turmeric and saffron will colour food yellow, but you can also buy a vegetable colouring that has no taste. Red food colouring is used for tandoori chicken.

Fennel (Soonf)

Small oval seeds, greenish and with an aniseed flavour, these have digestive properties, and are sometimes served roasted at the end of an Indian meal. Used sparingly, they give warmth and sweetness to curries.

Fenugreek (Methi)

These tawny-coloured seeds are chunky and very hard. Their bitter taste and aroma is released only by cooking. In powdered form, fenugreek is one of the main ingredients of curry powder. It is used sparingly on its own. The leaves of the plant, which is related to spinach, are used in India as a herb.

Garam masala

Garam masala, meaning "hot spices", is a mixture of ground spices that is used sparingly, sprinkled either on a finished dish or onto the food just before it has finished cooking. It is far better to grind your own spices than to buy the mixture ready-ground. Bought garam masala often contains inferior-quality spices and will not keep its flavour for long.

For home-made garam masala, grind together the cardamom seeds from 10 pods, 25 g (1 oz) cinnamon stick, 6 cloves and 6–8 whole black peppercorns. Store in an airtight jar in a cool place. (For preparing garam masala, see page 17.)

Ghee

This is clarified butter and can be made at home (see page 16). The advantage of using ghee is that it can be heated to a very high temperature without burning, and so is useful for browning onions in order to give a sauce a good rich colour, and for sizzling spices before the main ingredients are added to the pan. As the milk solids have been removed from ghee, it will keep well without being refrigerated. Many people prefer to use unsaturated fats and oils instead of ghee or butter.

Ginger

You can buy ginger ground (soondth) or fresh (adrak). The ground type is the same as that used in baking. The fresh "root" ginger is actually a rhizome, and is fawn in colour and knobbly. Inside, the ginger is hard, yellow and fibrous. It is easiest to cook with, once peeled and grated. You can also chop it if you are going to liquidise it with other ingredients. Fresh ginger can be kept wrapped in foil in the freezer or in a pot of sandy soil, kept fairly dry. It has quite a hot pungent flavour and should be used sparingly.

Mango powder (Amchur)

Unripe mangoes are sliced and dried, then powdered and sold as amchur. Amchur has a tart taste. If you are unable to find it, use a dash of lemon or lime instead.

Mustard seeds (Rai)

There are both white and black mustard seeds – the black contain a higher proportion of the volatile mustard oil. When dropped into hot oil, the mustard seeds pop, releasing their flavour. It is best to put a lid over the saucepan while you do this, or they will fly all over the kitchen. You can use this technique when shallow-frying Western food to add extra aroma.

Nutmeg and mace (Jaiphal and Javitri)

Mace is the fleshy lattice-like covering of the nutmeg, which is golden brown in colour. It is sold whole or powdered. Nutmegs are best bought whole and freshly grated at home.

Oil

Mustard oil, derived from the seeds of the mustard plant, is very popular with south Indian cooks, especially for pickling. This, and coconut oil, can be bought at specialist Indian shops. Coconut oil is stirred together with a little warm water to release its aroma before use.

Groundnut oil, also called arachide oil, is suitable for Indian cookery, as is the oil labelled simply "vegetable oil".

Paprika

Paprika is the ground seeds from the capsicum or sweet pepper. It is milder than chilli powder or cayenne.

Peppercorns (Mirchi)

Peppercorns grow on large bushes in Malabar, on the west coast of India. They are picked by hand just before they are ripe, when they are still green, then left in the sun to dry and become black and crinkly. White peppercorns are the mature fruit, left to ripen on the bush, with the outer husk removed. This is traditionally done by immersing sacks of peppercorns in running streams. Bacteria get to work and loosen the husks and the water finishes the job. The peppercorns are then trodden in vats, like grapes, to rid them of the final traces of husk.

Black pepper is more aromatic; white pepper is stronger and hotter. Black pepper should always be bought whole and freshly ground over your food as it loses its aroma quickly.

Poppy seeds (Khus-khus)

It is the milky juice in the poppy's seed pod from which opium is derived – the seeds themselves have no narcotic properties. They are small, black and hard. There is also a white type.

Saffron (Zaffran)

Saffron is the most expensive spice of all. It is the filaments from a specially cultivated crocus – 75,000 stamens are needed to make 100 g (4 oz) of the spice. It is grown in Kashmir and used on festive occasions to give food a bright yellow colour and a distinctive aroma. The filaments can be lightly roasted, crumbled in a little hot water and left to infuse to bring out their full strength. Buy saffron only from a reputable spice dealer or you may get an adulterated product, or something that is not saffron at all, especially if you buy it ready-powdered.

Sambar powder

This is a delicious aromatic spice mix used in a number of recipes in this book.

100 g (4 oz) coriander seeds
1 tsp asafoetida
4 whole red chillies
6 curry leaves
25 g (1 oz) polished split black lentils (urid dal)
25 g (1 oz) channa dal
25 g (1 oz) fenugreek seeds
1 tbsp mustard seeds
4–6 whole black peppercorns

Roast together the first four ingredients and set them aside. Then roast each of the remaining ingredients separately. (Some take very little roasting before the fragrance emerges and would burn if roasted with the rest). Now grind all the roasted spices together to a fine powder and store in a screw-top jar.

Tamarind (Amli)

A tamarind looks a little like a cinnamon-coloured pod of broad beans. It grows on tall trees and is peeled and seeded when ripe. The fruit is then squashed into bricks and this is how you buy it. It has a very tart citric flavour and if you cannot find it, use a dash of lemon or lime instead. (For preparing tamarind juice, see page 16.)

Turmeric (Haldi)

Turmeric is a rhizome related to ginger. Bought as a powder, it gives curries their characteristic golden yellow colour. It has a delicate taste and is mildly antiseptic, although it becomes bitter if too much is used. Indians often use turmeric with beans because of its digestive properties.

Vindaloo paste

This is a very hot spicy paste. Chillies may be used with their seeds if you like particularly fiery food. In western India the Christians eat pork vindaloo. For those not permitted pork, vindaloo goes well with beef, lamb or prawns.

10 red chillies
50 g (2 oz) fresh ginger, finely grated
12 cloves garlic, 4 chopped and 8 thinly sliced
½ tsp fenugreek seeds
1 tsp mustard seeds
1 tsp cumin seeds
2–3 tbsp white wine vinegar
5–6 tbsp oil
225 g (8 oz) onion, chopped
450 g (1 lb) tomatoes
peeled cardamom seeds from 8 pods

Grind or pound the chillies, half of the ginger, chopped garlic, fenugreek, mustard and cumin, and mix them to a paste with the vinegar. Do not add any water. Heat the oil and fry the onion until golden, then add the tomatoes and squash them into a paste as you cook. Stir in the spicy vinegar paste you have already made, add the remaining spices and fry until the oil runs out of them. The paste is then ready. Allow it to cool and store in an airtight container in a cool dark place.

Pulses (Dals)

There are many varieties of pulse available in India and most of them can be found in Britain at Indian grocery stores and health-food shops. Ahar dal, also called toor or toovar dal, is the main dal used in south India.

Moong dal *(Small, yellow, split pulses)* Beansprouts are made by sprouting these beans.

Masoor dal *(Split red pulses)* Salmon-coloured, small, flat, round pulses which cook easily.

Channa dal These are similar to split peas, but slightly smaller.

Rajma *(Red kidney beans)* Large, dark red kidney-shaped beans. Should be soaked overnight to reduce cooking time.

Urid dal *(Black gram)* The bean is reddish-black in colour, is very small in size and takes a long time to cook. The split urid dal is pale cream in colour. It is usually soaked and ground to a paste.

Lobia *(Black-eyed peas)* White, kidney-shaped beans with a black "eye". Popular in the north.

Mater *(Split peas)* Round, yellow pulses which are uniform in size.

Chole *(Chickpeas)* Beige, round, dried peas. Should be soaked overnight to reduce the cooking time. Chickpea flour is called gram, and is widely used in cooking.

Green moong dal *(Green lentils)* One of the more commonly used lentils. It can be used whole, split or polished to make various dals.

Special techniques

Adding spices to hot oil *(Baghar phoron)*
Oil is heated until it is very hot, and whole spices, crushed garlic or green chillies are added until the spices swell up or splutter or change colour. This is then added to a cooked dish, or vegetables, or other spices are added and cooking continues.

Dry roasting Place whole spices in a small, heavy-based frying pan and heat gently, stirring the spices constantly so that they do not burn. Soon the spices will turn a few shades darker and a lovely aroma will emerge.

Frying onions Place the oil in a frying pan or saucepan over a medium high heat. When hot add the onions, and, stirring occasionally, fry until the onions start to change colour. Lower the heat and continue to fry until they are reddish brown.

Adding yoghurt while cooking When a recipe calls for yoghurt, always whisk the yoghurt until smooth and add slowly, otherwise it curdles.

Peeling tomatoes Place the tomatoes in boiling water for 30 seconds. Drain and cool under running cold water. Peel, chop and use as required.

Cleaning chillies Pull out or slice off the stalks of the chillies and, holding them under cold running water, slit them open with a sharp knife and remove the seeds. The seeds are the hottest part of the chillies and most Indians do not remove them. Be very careful, when handling chillies, not to put your hands near your eyes as the oil will make your eyes burn.

Chillies can be stored for 12–14 days by removing the stalk of each chilli and putting them in a closed bottle in the fridge. When needed, wash the chillies and use as required.

SHELLING PISTACHIO NUTS

1 Pour boiling water over the nuts and leave for 30 seconds.

2 Drain and immerse in cold water.

3 The skin now peels away quite easily.

CLEANING A CHILLI

1 Slice off the stalk end of the chilli and hold it under cold running water. With a sharp knife, slit it open from top to bottom.

2 Remove all the seeds, keeping the chilli under the running water to prevent the oil splashing into your eyes.

MAKING COCONUT MILK

1 Add hot water to the grated coconut.

2 Blend the mixture until it is very smooth.

3 Pour through a sieve and collect the milk.

4 Squeeze the remaining milk out by hand.

Basic Recipes

Home-made Cottage Cheese (Paneer)

3.5 litres (6¼ pt) milk
about 250 ml (8 fl oz) warm water
about 5 tbsp white vinegar

When adding the water and vinegar mixture to the milk, do not add more than necessary as this tends to harden the paneer. Use in savoury or sweet dishes.

MAKING PANEER

1 Bring the milk to the boil and slowly add the water and vinegar.

2 Stop adding vinegar as soon as the milk curdles.

3 Strain the curdled milk through several layers of cloth.

4 Tie the ends of the cloth and squeeze the liquid out.

5 Hang the cheese up to drain.

Yoghurt
(Dahi)

Yoghurt is used a great deal in Indian cookery to marinate meats and to give flavour to certain types of curry.

As yoghurt is very refreshing and cool it is eaten at most meals in certain parts of the country, particularly in the north. It is eaten either plain or with some seasoning or vegetables added to it. In Bengal, sweetened yoghurt is eaten as a pudding.

On a hot day it can be mixed with water to make a refreshing drink called lassi.

Most families in India make their own yoghurt at home, though it is easily available in the shops.

> 1.2 litres (2 pt) milk
> 2½ tbsp yoghurt

1 Bring the milk to the boil, stirring constantly.
2 Remove the heat and let it cool so that it feels just warm.
3 Place the yoghurt in a large bowl and whisk until smooth. Slowly add the lukewarm milk and stir gently. Cover the bowl and leave in a warm place overnight. Chill and use as required.

Once you have made some yoghurt you can keep a little aside for the next batch, if you are going to make it within a day or two.

Clarified Butter
(Ghee)

> 450 g (1 lb) unsalted butter

Ghee can be bought at any Indian grocery store, but home-made ghee has a special flavour.

1 Heat the butter in a saucepan over a low heat. Let it simmer until all the white residue turns golden and settles at the bottom.
2 Remove from the heat, strain and cool.
3 Pour into an airtight bottle and store in a cool place.

Keeps for 1–2 months.

Tamarind Juice
(Imli Ki Rus)

> 75 g (3 oz) dried tamarind
> 250 ml (8 fl oz) hot water

1 Soak the tamarind in the water for about 30 minutes.
2 Squeeze the pulp well to draw out all the juice. Strain and use as required.

By altering the amount of water you can change the consistency.

Onion Mix
(Masala Mix)

2 large onions
3 tomatoes
3.5 cm (1½ in) ginger
5 cloves garlic
3–4 green chillies
4 tsp white vinegar

1 Blend all the ingredients together until you have a smooth paste.
2 Pour into an airtight bottle and keep in the fridge until needed. It will keep for up to two weeks.

Mixed Spice
(Garam Masala)

3 tbsp cardamom seeds
3 x 2.5 cm (1 in) pieces of cinnamon stick
1½ tsp cumin seeds
½ tbsp black peppercorns
½ tsp cloves
¼ of a nutmeg

1 Grind all the spices together until they are finely ground.
2 Store in a spice bottle until required.

The ingredients may be added in different proportions to suit individual taste.

Coconut Milk
(Narial Ki Dudh)

When buying a coconut, shake it to make sure it is full of water. The more liquid it has, the fresher it is. (This liquid is not coconut milk, it is coconut water, and can be served as a drink when chilled.)

To open the coconut Take a screwdriver and punch two holes in the eyes of the coconut and drain off all the liquid. Place in a preheated oven at 190°C/375°F/ Gas Mark 5 for 15–20 minutes. While the coconut is still hot, hit it with a hammer to split it and the flesh should come away from the shell.

To grate Peel off the brown skin from the coconut flesh and grate either with a hand grater or in a food processor.

To make coconut milk Combine the grated coconut with 500 ml (18 fl oz) of very hot water and blend. Pass this liquid through a sieve and squeeze the pulp to draw out all the liquid. This is known as thick coconut milk. The pulp is normally thrown away, but a few recipes may call for thin coconut milk, in which case the process is repeated using about 500 ml (18 fl oz) of hot water added to the coconut pulp. Blend the mixture and strain.

Thick milk has a lot more flavour than thin milk.

A quick method of making coconut milk is to blend together 75 g (3 oz) of creamed coconut with 500 ml (18 fl oz) of hot water. Creamed coconut is available in supermarkets in 200 g (7 oz) slabs. It keeps in the fridge for 2–3 months.

Roast Cumin
(Sukha Bhuna Jeera)

2 tbsp whole cumin seeds

1 Place the cumin seeds in a small saucepan over a medium heat and dry roast them, stirring constantly. The seeds will then turn a few shades darker. (Take care not to burn them.)
2 Cool and grind finely. Store in a spice bottle until required.

Coriander seeds and dried red chillies can be roasted and ground in a similar manner and stored.

The Indian kitchen

Indian food can be cooked easily in a modern kitchen and you do not need to go out and buy a lot of equipment. However, you may be interested to know about some of the more traditional implements and utensils of the Indian kitchen.

Chula This is a hollow cube with a hole towards the bottom through which fuel is fed, and a hole at the top which acts as the gas burner. Midway there are four or five iron rods which act as a bracket to hold the coal. The chula must have mud placed regularly on the inside and outside, so that it does not lose its shape. The mud is then left to dry out. There is a special technique to placing the mud, to ensure that after it dries out there are no cracks. In the cities, gas or electric cookers are often used instead.

Degchi This is a saucepan without handles, made of polished brass, stainless steel or other metals. The lid of the degchi is slightly dipped so that sometimes live coal can be placed on it to cook food slowly or keep food warm. Ordinary saucepans with lids can be used in the same way and the oven can be used to cook food slowly or to keep it warm.

Karai This is found in every Indian kitchen. It is a deep, concave metallic dish with two handles – one on each side. It looks like a Chinese wok but it is a little more rounded. It is used for deep frying. A deep fryer or saucepan or frying pan can be used if you do not have a karai.

Tava This is made from cast iron, is slightly concave, and is about 25 cm (10 in) in diameter. It is ideal for making chappatis or parathas as it distributes the heat evenly. A heavy-based frying pan will serve the same purpose.

Tongs These are used to remove a karai from the fire, or to remove the hot lid from the degchi. To remove the degchi from the fire it is normally held at either side with a cloth.

Metallic stirrers These are used in India as the pans are not non-stick. Use wooden spoons when using non-stick pans. Wooden spoons are easier to use as they do not get hot, although if left in hot oil they tend to burn.

Below: Modern kitchen equipment, such as a food processor, garlic press and stainless steel knives, can be put to good use in the preparation of many Indian dishes.

Thick stone slab This is used with a round stone roller like a rolling pin for grinding. Whole spices are ground with a little water; if dry ground spice is required a mortar and pestle is used. Pulses are also ground on the slab.

Tandoor This is a clay oven used in northern India. Tandoori chicken, whole or in pieces, different kinds of breads and kebabs are baked in this oven. It is about 91 cm–1.2 m (3–4 ft) deep and about 60 cm (2 ft) wide on top with a hole of 30 cm (12 in) diameter through which the food is put for cooking. It is fuelled by wood and coal and intensive heat builds up inside. This oven has mud patted on the inside and outside and it must be allowed to dry out. The chicken or the kebabs are marinated and then skewered and placed in the tandoor; the intensity of the heat cooks a whole chicken in a matter of minutes.

When bread is baked in a tandoor, the dough is slapped onto the inside of the oven and when bubbles form, which is in a matter of a few seconds, the bread is cooked. It does not need to be turned over.

Tandoori chicken can be cooked easily in the modern oven, and then put under a very hot grill for a few minutes to dry out. It can also taste excellent barbecued.

Electric coffee grinder In the modern kitchen, this can be used to grind spices. A blender or food processor may be used to blend onions, pulses and rice. The food processor can be used to make the dough for most of the breads and to save time when grating vegetables.

Below: Traditional kitchen equipment includes the karai, shown on the left of the picture with tongs to lift it from the heat and a wooden stirrer. The heavy frying pan and saucepan on the right of the are suitable modern substitutes for the tava and the degchi.

PULSES

India has over 60 varieties of pulses, which provide a primary source of protein for her millions of vegetarians. When cooked, they can be left whole or puréed, making them extremely versatile as ingredients for curries, stuffings and patties. They can even be roasted or deep-fried for garnishes or snacks. To cook pulses, first pick them over and remove any foreign bodies. The larger varieties should be soaked overnight (at least 10 hours). If you are in a hurry, you can bring them to the boil, continue boiling for a couple of minutes and then take the saucepan off the heat and leave it to stand for an hour before cooking.

Lentils with Vegetables I
(Kootu)

Serves 4
225 g (8 oz) toovar dal, washed
900 ml (1½ pt) water
½ tsp turmeric
1 tsp salt
75 g (3 oz) carrots, scraped and diced
50 g (2 oz) peas (fresh or frozen)
100 g (4 oz) French beans, cut into
    2.5 cm (1 in) lengths
I tbsp oil
1 tbsp urid dal
I tsp peppercorns
2 dried red chillies, broken in half
10–12 curry leaves
4 tbsp grated coconut
1 75 ml (6 fl oz) milk

Urid dal (*Black gram*) The bean is reddish-black in colour, is very small in size and takes a long time to cook. The split urid dal is pale cream in colour. It is usually soaked and ground to a paste.

1   Place the toovar dal, water, turmeric and salt in a saucepan and bring to the boil. Cover and simmer for about 35–40 minutes until the dal is soft. Add the vegetables and continue to cook until they are tender.
2   Whilst the toovar dal is being cooked, heat the oil in a small saucepan and fry the urid dal, peppercorns, red chillies, curry leaves and coconut until the dal and coconut turn golden. Grind to a paste.
3   When the dal and vegetables are cooked, add the paste and milk and continue to cook for 5–10 minutes. Serve hot with rice.

Lentils Flavoured with Garlic
(Rasam)

Serves 2
100 g (4 oz) toovar dal
900 ml (1½ pt) water
pinch of ground turmeric
1 tsp salt
2¼ tsp cumin seeds
1 tsp coriander seeds
½ tsp peppercorns
3–4 diced red chillies
250 ml (8 fl oz) tamarind juice (see page 16)
15 curry leaves
5 cloves garlic, crushed
1 tomato, chopped
1 tsp ghee (see page 16)

1   Wash the toovar dal in several changes of water and bring to the boil in a large saucepan with the measured amount of water, turmeric and salt. Cover, leaving the lid slightly open, and simmer for about 30 minutes until the dal is soft. Blend until smooth.
2   In the meantime, dry roast 2tspcumin, coriander, peppercorns and red chillies and grind finely.
3   Mix the tamarind juice, the powdered spices, 10 curry leaves and garlic and bring to the boil. Simmer until it has reduced by half.
4   Add the cooked dal and tomato and simmer for 5 minutes.
5   In a small saucepan, heat the ghee until very hot, add the ¼ tsp of cumin seeds and the remaining curry leaves and let them sizzle for 5–6 seconds. Add to the cooked dal. Serve very hot with rice or as a soup.

Special Curried Chickpeas
(Channa Curry)

Serves 4

225 g (8 oz) chickpeas
1.2 litres (2 pt) water
½ tsp bicarbonate of soda
100 g (4 oz) butter or ghee
1 onion
2 or 3 bay leaves
cardamom seeds from 1 pod
2.5 cm (1 in) cinnamon stick
3 cloves
15 g (½ oz) fresh ginger, finely grated
1 tsp fennel seeds
3 cloves garlic, chopped
175 g (6 oz) tomatoes, peeled and chopped
1 tsp chilli powder
1½ tsp ground cumin
leaves from 1–2 sprigs coriander
½ tsp paprika
2 tsp ground coriander
1 tbsp lemon juice
salt

1   Pick over the chickpeas and wash thoroughly. Soak in water for at least 10 hours. Drain and cook in the measured water with the bicarbonate of soda for 1½ hours, depending on the age of the peas, until tender but not soft.
2   Heat three-quarters of the butter or ghee in a good-sized saucepan and add the onion, bay leaves, cardamom seeds, cinnamon, cloves, ginger, fennel seeds, garlic and tomatoes. Fry until the onion is golden, squashing the tomato under the back of a wooden spoon to make a thick paste.
3   Add the chilli powder, half the cumin, the coriander leaves and paprika and cook for 3–4 minutes, stirring occasionally.
4   Add the cooked chickpeas with about 120 ml (4 fl oz) of their cooking liquor and cook over a low heat for 8–10 minutes.
5   In a separate pan, heat the remaining butter or ghee and when hot, add the remaining ground cumin. Fry for a few seconds, until the fragrance emerges, and add to the chickpeas.
6   Sprinkle on the ground coriander and lemon juice, and add salt to taste.

Steamed Rice and Lentil Cakes
(Idli)

Serves 4

90 g (2½ oz) urid dal, washed
200 g (7 oz) rice, washed
good pinch of baking powder
pinch of salt

1 Soak the dal and rice separately in plenty of water for 4–5 hours. Drain.
2 In a liquidiser or food processor, grind the dal to a fine paste, adding a little water if necessary.
3 Grind the rice coarsely, adding a little water if necessary.
4 Mix the dal and rice together thoroughly, cover and then leave in a warm place overnight to let them ferment.
5 Mix in the baking powder and salt.
6 Fill the idli vessel* with the fermented mixture and steam for about 10 minutes until an inserted skewer comes out clean.

☙ *If you do not have an idli vessel, you can use egg poachers.*

Lentils with Vegetables II
(Sambar)

Serves 4

225 g (8 oz) toovar dal, washed	350 g (12 oz) aubergine, cut into 1 cm (½ in) pieces
1 litre (1¾ pt) water	
2 tsp salt	90 g (2½ oz) French beans, cut into 4 cm (1½ in) lengths
½ tsp ground turmeric	
1½ tbsp oil	
4 tsp coriander seeds	6–8 shallots, peeled
1 tsp channa dal	120 ml (4 fl oz) tamarind juice (see page 16)
1 tsp urid dal	
6 dried red chillies	
pinch of fenugreek seeds	1 tsp mustard seeds
good pinch of asafoetida	8–10 curry leaves

1 Place the toovar dal, water, 1 tsp of salt and turmeric in a large saucepan and bring to the boil. Lower the heat, cover, leaving the lid slightly ajar, and simmer for 35–40 minutes until the dal is soft.
2 In the meantime, heat ½ tbsp of oil in a small saucepan and fry the coriander seeds, channa dal and urid dal, 4 dried red chillies, fenugreek and asafoetida, stirring constantly, until golden. (Take care that they do not get burnt.) Grind to a fine powder.
3 When the dal is soft, add the vegetables, tamarind juice and the remaining salt and continue to simmer until the vegetables are nearly tender.
4 Add the ground spices, stir well and cook for 5 minutes. Remove from the heat and put aside.
5 Heat the remaining 1 tbsp of oil in a small saucepan until very hot, add the mustard seeds and, when they stop spluttering, add the remaining dried red chillies, broken in half, and the curry leaves and let them fry for 4–5 seconds. Add this to the hot dal, give it a good stir and serve.

Stuffed, Spiced Pastries
(Kachori)

Serves 4

Filling

100 g (4 oz) urid dal, washed
1 tsp ghee (see page 16)
1 tsp salt
¼ tsp fennel seeds
1 cm (½ in) cinnamon stick
½ black cardamom pod, skinned
6 peppercorns
pinch of asafoetida
pinch of ground ginger
¼ tsp ground cumin
½ tsp chilli powder

Dough

225 g (8 oz) wholewheat flour
1 tsp salt
2 tsp ghee (see page 16)
120 ml (4 fl oz) hot water
oil for deep frying

1 To make the filling, soak the dal in plenty of cold water overnight.
2 Drain and blend to a smooth paste, adding a little water if necessary.
3 Heat the ghee in a karai, add the dal paste and salt and, stirring constantly, fry until the mixture leaves the side and forms a lump. Keep on one side.
4 Grind together the fennel, cinnamon, black cardamom and peppercorns to a fine powder.
5 Add this and all the remaining spices to the dal and mix.
6 To make the dough, mix the wholewheat flour and salt.
7 Rub the ghee into the flour/salt mixture.
8 Add enough hot water to make a soft, pliable dough. Knead for about 10 minutes.
9 Divide the dough into 12–14 balls.
10 Take one ball, flatten slightly and make a depression in the middle with your thumb, to form a cup shape. Fill the centre with the spiced dal mixture and re-form the pastry ball, making sure that the edges are well gathered. Flatten the ball slightly between the palms of your hands.
11 Heat the oil in a karai over a medium heat and fry the kachoris a few at a time for 7–8 minutes until they are lightly browned. Serve with pickles.

Fried Lentil Cake Curry
(Dhokkar Dalna)

Serves 4

150 g (5 oz) channa dal, soaked overnight in 900 ml (1½ pt) water and drained
¾ tsp salt
½ tsp ground turmeric
1 cm (½ in) ginger, grated
2 tbsp desiccated coconut
2 green chillies
150 ml (¼ pt) water
200 ml (⅓ pt) oil
3 medium potatoes, cut into 2.5 cm (1 in) pieces
½ tsp whole cumin seeds
2 bay leaves
1 tsp ground turmeric
½ tsp chilli powder
1½ tsp ground cumin
1 tsp ground coriander
½ tsp salt
2 tomatoes, chopped
350 ml (12 fl oz) water
1 tsp ghee
½ tsp garam masala (see page 17)

1 Mix the drained dal with ¾ tsp salt, ½ tsp turmeric, ginger, coconut, green chillies and 150 ml (¼ pt) water in a blender until you have a smooth creamy mixture.

2 In a karai, heat 120 ml (4 fl oz) of the oil over medium heat and fry the dal mixture until it leaves the sides and a ball forms. Spread 1 cm (½ in) thick on a greased plate. Cool. Cut into 2.5 cm (1 in) squares.

3 Heat the rest of the oil in a karai over medium high heat and fry the dal squares a few at a time until golden brown. Set aside.

4 Fry the potatoes until lightly browned. Set aside.

5 Lower the heat to medium, add the whole cumin seeds and bay leaves and let them sizzle for a few seconds.

6 Add the turmeric, chilli, cumin, coriander, salt and tomatoes and fry for 2 minutes. Add the water and bring to boil.

7 Add the potatoes, cover and cook for 10 minutes. Add the fried dal squares, cover again and cook until the potatoes are tender.

8 Add the ghee and sprinkle on garam masala. Remove from the heat. Serve hot with rice or pillau.

Lentils cooked with Fish Heads
(Mooror Dal)

Serves 4
225 g (8 oz) green lentils
about 1.5 litre (2½ pt) water
¼ tsp ground turmeric
1 tsp salt
4 tbsp oil
2 fish heads, quartered
3 green chillies,
2 dried red chillies
1 medium onion, chopped
¼ tsp chilli powder
4 cardamom pods
5 cm (2 in) cinnamon stick
2 bay leaves
good pinch of sugar

1 Dry roast the pulses, stirring constantly, until golden brown.
2 Wash the pulses in several changes of water. Bring the pulses to a boil in the measured amount of water with the turmeric and salt.
3 Throw away the scum, lower the heat, cover, leaving the lid slightly open, and simmer for about 1 hour. Put aside.
4 Heat the oil in a saucepan and fry the fish heads until golden brown.
5 Drain the fish heads and add to the pulses. Put the remaining oil aside. Bring the pulses to the boil again, add the green chillies, lower the heat and simmer for about 15 minutes.
6 In a small pan, heat the remaining oil again until very hot. Add the dried red chillies and fry for 4–5 seconds. Add the onion and stirfry until golden brown.
7 Add the chilli powder, cardamom, cinnamon, bay leaves and sugar and fry for a few seconds.
8 Add to the pulses and stir thoroughly.

Curried Chickpeas with Coconut
(Channa Curry)

Serves 4
225 g (8 oz) chickpeas
4–5 tbsp butter or ghee
1 tsp mustard seeds
1 onion, finely chopped
1 tbsp finely grated fresh ginger
1 green chilli, chopped
4–6 curry leaves
75 g (3 oz) grated fresh coconut
salt

1 Pick over the chickpeas, wash thoroughly and soak in water for at least 10 hours. Cook in fresh water for 1–1½ hours, depending on the age of the chickpeas, until tender but not soft.
2 Heat the butter or ghee in a saucepan and add the mustard seeds. Let them sizzle for a few seconds until they have all popped.
3 Add the onion and fry until golden.
4 Drain the chickpeas, reserving the cooking liquor. Add the chickpeas to the saucepan with the ginger, green chilli and about 2 tbsp cooking liquor. Cover and cook over low heat, stirring occasionally, for 10 minutes, until the chickpeas have absorbed the flavours of the sauce.
5 Stir in the curry leaves and grated coconut and add salt to taste.

Dal Curry I

Serves 2
175 g (6 oz) toovar dal
900 ml (1½ pt) water
2 tbsp oil
½ tsp mustard seeds
½ tsp cumin seeds
1 small onion, finely chopped
leaves from 1–2 sprigs coriander
2 tomatoes, peeled and chopped
½ tsp turmeric
1 clove garlic, finely chopped
2 green chillies, sliced
salt

1 Pick over the dal and wash it well. Bring the water to the boil, add the dal and simmer for about 15 minutes, until you can crush the dal with the back of a wooden spoon. Set aside, covered.
2 Heat the oil in a frying pan and add the mustard seeds. Sizzle for a few seconds until all the seeds have popped.
3 Add the cumin seeds, onion and half the coriander leaves and fry, stirring, until the onion is golden.
4 Add the tomato, turmeric, garlic and chilli, stirring well and mashing the tomato with the spices to make a paste.
5 Add the dal with a little of its cooking water. Stir well, heat through and add salt to taste. Garnish with the remaining coriander leaves.

Dal and Mushroom Curry (Kumban Dal)

Serves 4
225 g (8 oz) red lentils (masoor dal)
1.2 l (2 pt) water
1½ tsp turmeric
175–225 g (6–8 oz) button mushrooms, halved
15 g (½ oz) fresh ginger, finely grated
1 green chilli, sliced
225 g (8 oz) onion, chopped
1 tbsp sambar powder (see page 11)
2 tbsp grated or desiccated coconut
225 g (8 oz) tomatoes, peeled and chopped
2 tbsp oil
1 tsp mustard seeds
4–6 curry leaves
salt

1 Pick over the dal and wash it thoroughly. Cook in the water with the turmeric for 10–15 minutes, until it can be crushed under the back of a wooden spoon.
2 Add the mushrooms, ginger, chilli and half of the onion, and cook for a further 10 minutes.
3 Meanwhile, blend the sambar powder with the coconut in a liquidiser, add to the curry with the tomato and cook for a further 6–8 minutes, until the sauce is thick and smooth.
4 Heat the oil in a pan, add the mustard seeds and let them sizzle for a few seconds until they have all popped.
5 Add the curry leaves and remaining onion and fry until the onion is golden. Add to the curry with salt to taste.

Dal Curry II

Serves 4

350 g (12 oz) toovar dal
1.2 litres (2 pt) boiling water
50 g (2 oz) butter or ghee
1 green pepper, sliced
½ tsp cumin seeds
1–2 green chillies, chopped
   1½ tbsp gram (chickpea) flour
salt
leaves from 1 sprig of coriander, finely chopped

1 Pick over the dal and wash it well. Add to the water and simmer for 10–15 minutes until soft. Strain off excess water and mash well or blend in a liquidiser. Set aside.
2 Heat the butter or ghee in a pan and when hot, fry the green pepper until soft. Add the cumin seeds and green chilli for a few seconds until their flavour emerges. Add to the dal.
3 In a small bowl, mix the gram flour with 2–3 tbsp water until it forms a smooth paste.
4 Stir the paste into the dal and simmer on a low heat, stirring occasionally, for about 5 minutes, until it is thick and soupy.
5 Stir in salt to taste and garnish with coriander.

Red Lentils with Fried Onions
(Masoor Dal)

Serves 2

200 g (7 oz) red lentils, washed
1 litre (1¾ pt) water
¼ tsp ground turmeric
1½ tsp ground cumin
2 tomatoes, chopped
½ tsp salt
2–3 green chillies
1 tbsp coriander leaves, chopped
3 tbsp ghee (see page 16)
3 cloves garlic, crushed
1 onion, finely sliced

1 Bring the lentils to the boil in the measured amount of water in a large saucepan. Remove any scum that forms.
2 Add the turmeric, cumin and tomatoes, and mix with the pulses.
3 Lower the heat, partially cover and simmer the lentils for about 40 minutes until tender. Add the salt, chillies and coriander leaves and mix in with the pulses. Remove from the heat.
4 In a small pan, heat the ghee. Add the garlic and onion and fry until golden brown.
5 Pour over the pulses and serve with rice.

Dal and Coconut Curry
(Dal Narial)

Serves 2

175 g (6 oz) toovar dal
900 ml (1½ pt) water
1½ tsp turmeric
½ tsp chilli powder
1 small onion, finely chopped
2–3 tbsp grated coconut
1 tomato, peeled and chopped
2 tbsp oil
1 tsp mustard seeds
4–6 curry leaves
salt

1 Pick over the dal and wash it well. Bring the water to the boil, add the dal and simmer for 10–15 minutes, until soft and mushy.
2 Stir in the turmeric and chilli powder, cover and keep hot over a low heat.
3 Put half the onion with the coconut in a liquidiser, add 1 tbsp water and blend until smooth. Stir into the dal with the tomato.
4 Heat the oil in a saucepan and add the mustard seeds. When all the seeds have popped, add the remaining onion and fry until golden. Add to the dal.
5 Stir in the curry leaves and salt to taste.

Green Lentil Curry I
(Moong Dal)

Serves 2

200 g (7 oz) whole green lentils (moong dal)
1.4 l (2½ pt) water
¼ tsp ground turmeric
1 tsp ground cumin
2 tomatoes, chopped
1 tsp salt
1 tbsp ghee (see page 16)
¾ tsp whole cumin seeds
2 dried red chillies
2 bay leaves
2.5 cm (1 in) cinnamon stick
4 green cardamom pods

1 Heat a saucepan and dry roast the lentils, stirring constantly until all the lentils turn light brown.
2 Wash the lentils in several changes of water and bring to boil in the measured amount of water in a large saucepan. Skim off any scum that forms.
3 Lower the heat, add the turmeric, cumin, tomatoes and salt and partially cover and simmer for about 1 hour 15 minutes until the lentils are soft.
4 In a small pan, heat the ghee over medium heat, add the cumin seeds, red chillies, bay leaves, cinnamon stick and cardamoms and let them sizzle for a few seconds.
5 Add the hot ghee and spices to the lentils and stir. Serve with rice.

Black-eyed Peas with Onions
(Lobia Aur Pyaz)

Serves 2

200 g (7 oz) black-eyed peas, washed
1.2 litres (2 pt) water
2 tbsp oil
1 large onion, finely chopped
2 cloves garlic, crushed
5 mm (¼ in) ginger, grated
1–2 green chillies, finely chopped
½ tsp salt
1 tsp treacle

1   Soak the beans in the water overnight.
2   Boil the beans in the water and then cover and simmer for 1 hour until tender. Drain.
3   Heat the oil in a large saucepan and fry the onion, garlic, ginger and chilli until the onions are soft.
4   Add the beans, salt and treacle and cook until all the moisture is absorbed, about 15 minutes. Serve with Chappatis (see page 106).

Spiced Chickpeas
(Masala Channa)

Serves 4

225 g (8 oz) chickpeas
100 g (4 oz) butter or ghee
1 onion, finely chopped
2 cloves garlic, finely chopped
1 tbsp finely grated fresh ginger
225 g (8 oz) peeled and chopped tomatoes
½ tsp ground coriander
½ tsp chilli powder
1 tbsp mango powder (amchur)
½ tsp ground cumin
1 tsp garam masala
leaves from 1 sprig of coriander
salt

1 Pick over the chickpeas, wash thoroughly and soak in water for at least 10 hours. Drain and cook in fresh water for 1–1½ hours, depending on the age of the chickpeas, until tender but not soft.
2 Heat the butter or ghee in a pan, add the onion, garlic and ginger and fry until the onion is golden.
3 Add the tomato, coriander, chilli, mango powder, cumin, garam masala and half of the coriander leaves. Cook, stirring briskly to mash the tomato with the back of the spoon into a paste.
4 Drain the chickpeas, reserving the cooking liquor, and add to the saucepan with 2 tbsp of the liquor. Cover and cook over low heat, stirring occasionally, for about 10 minutes, until the chickpeas have absorbed the flavours of the spices.
5 Sprinkle on the remaining coriander leaves and add salt to taste.

Soured Chickpeas
(Chole)

Serves 4

200 g (7 oz) chickpeas, washed
900 ml (1½ pt) water
1 teabag
3 tbsp oil
225 g (8 oz) potatoes, boiled and diced
    into 1 cm (½ in) cubes
2 medium onions, finely chopped
1 clove garlic, crushed
1 cm (½ in) ginger, grated
2 tsp ground coriander
2 green chillies, chopped
1½ tbsp mango powder (amchur)
½ tsp chilli powder
¾ tsp salt
175 ml (6 fl oz) water
1½ tsp garam masala (see page 17)

1 Soak the chickpeas in the water with the teabag overnight.
2 Discard the teabag and place the chickpeas and the water in a saucepan and bring to the boil. Cover and simmer for about 1 hour until tender. Drain.
3 Heat the oil in a saucepan over medium heat and fry the diced potatoes until lightly browned. Set aside.
4 In the remaining oil, fry the onions until golden brown. Add the garlic and ginger and fry a further 2 minutes.
5 Add the chickpeas, coriander, green chillies, mango powder, chilli, salt and potatoes and stir fry for about 2 minutes until well mixed.
6 Add the water and cook for about 15 minutes. Sprinkle with garam masala. Serve hot with Yoghurt Bread (see page 110).

Curried Red Kidney Beans
(Masala Rajma)

Serves 4
200 g (7 oz) red kidney beans, washed
1.2 litres (2 pt) water
6 tbsp oil
2 bay leaves
5 cm (2 in) cinnamon stick
3 green cardamom pods
1 large onion, finely sliced
2 cloves garlic, crushed
1 cm (½ in) ginger, grated
¾ tsp ground turmeric
½ tsp chilli powder
½ tsp salt
2 tomatoes, chopped
120 ml (4 fl oz) water

1   Soak the beans in the water overnight.
2   Boil the beans in the water and then cover and simmer for 1 hour until tender. Drain.
3   Heat the oil in a large saucepan over medium high heat and put in the bay leaves, cinnamon and cardamom pods and let them sizzle for a few seconds. Add the onion, garlic and ginger and fry until the onions are golden brown.
4   Add the turmeric, chilli, salt and tomatoes and fry for 1 minute. Add the drained beans and fry with the spices for 2–3 minutes.
5   Add 120 ml (4 fl oz) water and bring to the boil, stirring occasionally. Cover, lower heat and cook for 10–15 minutes. Serve with Chappatis (see page 106).

Whole Black Beans
(Mahan Ki Dal)

Serves 2
175 g (6 oz) whole black beans (sabut urid)
1 cm (½ in) ginger, grated
3 dried red chillies
4 cloves garlic, crushed
1½ tsp salt
1.5–1.75 litre (2½–3 pt) water
3 tbsp yoghurt, lightly beaten
4 tbsp ghee (see page 16)
1 small onion, chopped
1 tbsp coriander leaves, chopped

1   Wash the beans in several changes of water.
2   Place the beans, ginger, chillies, garlic, salt and water in a large saucepan and bring to the boil. Lower the heat, cover, leaving the lid slightly ajar, and simmer for about 3–3½ hours until the beans are soft. (Add further water if required.)
3   Mash the beans slightly and add the yoghurt and 1 tbsp of the ghee. Cook for a further 30 minutes. (When the beans are cooked they should turn reddish-brown in colour and the consistency should be thick.)
4   Heat the remaining ghee and fry the onion until lightly golden. Add this to the hot beans and garnish with the coriander leaves.

VEGETABLES

India grows a huge variety of vegetables, and the combinations of vegetables and spices are endless. Sometimes the spices are used to make a thick sauce, and at other times the vegetables are cooked "dry" *(toran)* so that the spices stick to them, making a tasty, crunchy "crust". Hot spicy vegetables are usually served with rice and mild fragrant ones with bread.

Ripe Mango Curry
(Aam Curry)

Serves 4

4 small sweet ripe mangoes, cubed,
   with the skins left on
600 ml (1 pt) water
2 tsp chilli powder
½ tsp turmeric
salt
grated flesh of ½ coconut
½ tsp ground cumin
6 curry leaves
2 tbsp oil
2 tsp mustard seeds
2 tsp fenugreek seeds
2 red chillies, cut into 4 pieces
2–3 tsp sugar

1. Cook the mango in the water with the chilli powder, turmeric and 1 tsp salt for about 5 minutes, making sure that the mango does not lose its shape.
2. Blend the coconut with the cumin and add to the mango with half the curry leaves.
3. Heat the oil in a frying pan and when hot, add the mustard seeds. Let them sizzle for a few seconds until they have all popped, then add the fenugreek seeds, red chilli and remaining curry leaves. Stir and fry for a few seconds, then add to the mango. Stir well and add sugar and salt to taste.

Buttermilk Curry
(Kalan)

Serves 4–6
225 g (8 oz) yam, peeled and cubed
1 green plantain, peeled and cubed
225 g (8 oz) white pumpkin, peeled and cubed
½ tsp turmeric
½ tsp chilli powder
grated flesh of 1 small coconut
½ tsp ground cumin
½ tsp ground white pepper
600 ml (1 pt) soured buttermilk, made by stirring
    3 tbsp water into 225 g (8 oz) yoghurt
2 green chillies, cut in half
2 tbsp oil
1 tsp mustard seeds
2 red chillies, cut into 3 or 4 pieces
½ tsp fenugreek seeds
8 curry leaves
2 tbsp sugar
2 tsp salt

1 Cook the yam, plantain and pumpkin in water to cover with the turmeric and chilli powder, over a low heat for about 10 minutes, until tender but not soft.
2 Blend the coconut, cumin and pepper and mix well with the buttermilk, then add to the saucepan with the vegetables and green chillies. Heat through on a low heat for 3–4 minutes, stirring briskly to prevent the buttermilk from separating.
3 Heat the oil in a pan, add the mustard seeds, red chilli, fenugreek seeds and half the curry leaves and let them sizzle for a few seconds, until all the seeds have popped.
4 Stir into the curry with the remaining curry leaves, and the sugar and salt to taste.

Stuffed Vegetables
(Sambharia)

Serves 4
2 long aubergines
6 small potatoes, peeled
6 small onions, peeled
5 green chillies
1 cm (½ in) ginger
175 g (6 oz) gram flour
1 tbsp ground coriander
½ tsp ground cumin
pinch of ground turmeric
1 tsp salt
¾ tsp sugar
about 120 ml (4 fl oz) oil
2 tbsp lime juice
¾ tsp mustard seeds
good pinch of asafoetida
2 tbsp coconut, grated
2 tbsp coriander leaves, chopped

1 Wash the vegetables and dry thoroughly.
2 Cut the aubergine into 4 cm (1½ in) slices.
3 Make 2 cuts crossways on each vegetable; cut about three-quarters of the way down the length, but do not cut right through.
4 Grind together 2 green chillies and the ginger to a paste.
5 Make a paste by mixing the gram flour, coriander, cumin, turmeric, salt, sugar, 2½ tbsp oil, lime juice and the chilli and ginger paste.
6 Carefully open the slits in the vegetables and stuff them with this paste. If you have any paste left over after stuffing the vegetables, add it to the vegetables while they are being fried.
7 In a large, heavy-based frying pan, heat the remaining oil, add 3 green chillies, broken in half, mustard and asafoetida and let them sizzle for 8–10 seconds.
8 Add the vegetables carefully, cover and fry over a low heat, occasionally stirring gently. When one side is done, turn the vegetables over, and cover and cook the second side. Add a little more oil if necessary. Serve hot, garnished with the coconut and coriander.

Mixed Vegetables
(Choch Chori)

Serves 4

1 medium potato, peeled	1 tsp panch phoron
200 g (7 oz) white radish, scraped	2 bay leaves
1 small aubergine	¾ tsp ground turmeric
225 g (8 oz) pumpkin, peeled	½ tsp chilli powder
275 g (10 oz) cauliflower stalks	½ tsp mustard seeds, ground
4 tbsp oil	½ tsp salt
2–3 dried red chillies, broken in half	½ tsp sugar
	120 ml (4 fl oz) water

1 Cut the potatoes into 8 pieces lengthways.
2 Quarter the white radish lengthways and cut into 4 cm (1½ in) lengths.
3 Cut off the stalk from the aubergine and quarter lengthways. Cut into 4 cm (1½ in) lengths.
4 Cut the pumpkin into 2.5 cm (1 in) cubes.
5 Cut the cauliflower stalks into very thin strips of 6 cm (2½ in) long.
6 Heat the oil in a karai or saucepan over a medium high heat, add the dried chillies and fry until they become brownish black (about 4–5 seconds).
7 Add the panch phoron and bay leaves and let them sizzle for a few seconds.
8 Add all the vegetables and fry for 3–4 minutes, stirring constantly.
9 Add the turmeric, chilli, mustard, salt and sugar and mix thoroughly with the vegetables.
10 Lower the heat to medium, cover and cook for 10 minutes.
11 Remove the cover, give the vegetables a good stir and then add the water. Bring to the boil, cover again and cook for about 10–15 minutes, until all the vegetables are tender and all the water has evaporated.
12 Serve with rice and Red Lentils with Fried Onions (page 30).

Vegetable Curry with Roast Coconut
(Eliseri)

Serves 2–3

100 g (4 oz) toovar dal
1.2 litres (2 pt) water
450 g (1 lb) pumpkin, cubed
1 tsp chilli powder
½ tsp turmeric
salt
50–75 g (2–3 oz) grated or desiccated coconut
1 tsp ground cumin
6–8 curry leaves
3 tbsp oil
1 tsp mustard seeds
2 red chillies, cut into pieces

1 Pick over the dal, wash it thoroughly and cook in the water for about 15 minutes, until you can mash it under the back of a wooden spoon.
2 Meanwhile, cook the pumpkin in water for about 12 minutes, until tender.
3 Drain the dal and the pumpkin, reserving a little of the cooking liquor, and mix the two together with the chilli, turmeric and ½ tsp salt. Cook over a low heat, stirring, for 3–4 minutes, adding a little of the cooing liquor if the mixture threatens to stick. Cover and set aside.
4 Blend half the coconut with the cumin and half the curry leaves. Stir into the curry.
5 Heat the oil in a frying pan and when hot, add the mustard seeds and red chilli. Let them sizzle for a few seconds until all the mustard seeds have popped. Add the remaining grated coconut and curry leaves and fry, stirring briskly, for a few seconds until the fragrance of roast coconut emerges.
6 Fold the fried spice mixture into the curry and add salt to taste.

Vegetable Curry with Coconut Milk
(Sabzi Narial)

Serves 4

flesh of 1 coconut, grated
450 g (1 lb) ripe pumpkin, peeled and sliced
2 carrots, peeled and sliced
1 tbsp coconut oil, mixed with 1 tbsp water
4–6 curry leaves
salt

1 Blend the coconut in a liquidiser with 1 tbsp boiling water. Transfer to a piece of muslin and squeeze out the milk into a bowl. Return the coconut to the liquidiser, add another tbsp boiling water and repeat the process, straining the milk into a separate bowl.
2 Cook the sliced pumpkin and carrots in water to cover on a low heat for about 10 minutes until tender, then add the second bowl of coconut milk and bring to the boil. Remove the saucepan from the heat.
3 Stir in the first bowl of coconut milk, add the coconut oil, curry leaves and salt to taste.

Vegetables in a Yoghurt and Coconut Sauce
(Avial)

Serves 4

2 plantains, peeled and cut into 1 cm (½ in) pieces
100 g (4 oz) green beans, cut into 1 cm (½ in) pieces
50 g (2 oz) carrots, diced into 5 mm (¼ in) cubes
50 g (2 oz) peas
¾ tsp chilli powder
½ tsp ground turmeric
¾ tsp salt
350 ml (12 fl oz) water
250 ml (8 fl oz) natural yoghurt
2 green chillies, chopped
1 tsp ground coriander
2 tbsp desiccated coconut
1 tbsp oil
½ tsp whole mustard seeds
6–8 curry leaves

1 Place the vegetables, chilli powder, turmeric, salt and water in a large saucepan and bring to the boil. Simmer for about 20 minutes until the vegetables are tender. Remove from the heat.
2 Whisk the yoghurt, green chillies, coriander and coconut together and set aside.
3 In a large saucepan heat the oil over medium high heat. Add the mustard seeds and curry leaves, and after 5–6 seconds add the vegetables with the liquid. Cook for 2–3 minutes. Lower the heat and add the yoghurt mixture and, stirring occasionally, cook for a further 4–5 minutes. Serve with rice.

Vegetable Curry, Kerala Style
(Sambar)

Serves 4–6

350 g (12 oz) toovar dal
1.2 litres (2 pt) water
½ tsp turmeric
100–175 g (4–6 oz) okra, trimmed and
   cut into 2.5 cm (1 in) lengths
3 tbsp oil
1 medium onion, quartered and sliced
225 g (8 oz) potatoes, cubed
2 tomatoes, peeled and chopped
2 tbsp tamarind juice (see page 16)
75–100 g (3–4 oz) grated coconut
4–6 curry leaves
2 tbsp sambar powder (see page 11)
1 tsp mustard seeds
1 red chilli, cut into 4 pieces
salt
coriander leaves, to garnish

1 Pick over the dal, wash it thoroughly and cook in the water with the turmeric for about 15 minutes, until you can mash it under the back of a wooden spoon.

2 Meanwhile, fry the okra in 1 tbsp oil, turning gently, until all the oil is absorbed. This seals the okra and helps it keep its shape. Set aside.

3 When the dal is ready, stir in the onion and potato and continue to cook gently on a low heat for about 8 minutes, until the vegetables are half-cooked.

4 Add the tomato and okra and cook for a further 10 minutes, until the vegetables are tender, adding a little extra water if the pot threatens to boil dry.

5 Stir in the tamarind juice, cover and keep hot.

6 Fry the coconut and half the curry leaves in 1 tbsp oil, then blend with the sambar powder and add to the vegetables.

7 Heat the remaining oil, add the mustard seeds and the red chilli and let them sizzle for a few seconds until all the mustard seeds have popped. Add to the curry.

8 Stir in salt to taste and garnish with coriander leaves.

Vegetable Curry, Tamil Style
(Sambar)

Serves 4–6

350 g (12 oz) toovar dal
1.2 litres (2 pt) water
1 aubergine
2 medium potatoes
1 medium onion, quartered and sliced
½ tsp turmeric
salt
3–4 tbsp tamarind juice (see page 16)
3 tbsp sambar powder (see page 11)
1 tomato, cut into 8 pieces
1 tbsp oil
1 tsp mustard seeds
4–6 curry leaves
2 tsp sugar
leaves from 1 sprig of coriander

1 Pick over the dal, wash it thoroughly and cook in the water for about 15 minutes, until you can mash it under the back of a wooden spoon.
2 Meanwhile, peel the aubergine and potatoes and cut into cubes, dropping them in a saucepan of water as you go to prevent discolouration.
3 Add the aubergine, potato and onion to the cooked dal, with a little extra water if necessary, and cook for about 8 minutes, until the vegetables are half-cooked.
4 Add the turmeric and ½ tsp salt, and continue cooking for about 10 minutes, until the vegetables are tender.
5 Stir in the tamarind juice, sambar powder and tomato, cover and keep hot.
6 Heat the oil in a saucepan and add the mustard seeds and curry leaves. Let them sizzle for a few seconds, until all the mustard seeds have popped, then add to the curry.
7 Stir in sugar and salt to taste and garnish with coriander leaves.

Spicy Mustard Leaves
(Sarson Ki Saag)

Serves 4

450 g (1 lb) mustard leaves
225 g (8 oz) spinach
2–3 green chillies, chopped
1 tsp salt
120 ml (4 fl oz) water
about 2 tbsp cornflour
2 tbsp ghee
1 onion, finely chopped
1 cm (½ in) ginger, grated
4 cloves garlic, crushed
4 tbsp butter

1 Wash the greens and chop finely.
2 Place the greens, chillies, salt and water in a large saucepan and cook on a low heat, stirring occasionally. A lot of water is given out by the greens, but if all the moisture dries up before the greens are cooked, add a little more water. Cook until the greens are tender and all the moisture has evaporated.
3 Place this mixture in a food processor or liquidiser and blend to a purée without adding any more water.
4 After blending, add enough cornflour and mix into the purée to the desired consistency.
5 Heat the ghee in a large frying pan, add the onion, ginger and garlic and fry until lightly golden.
6 Add the puréed greens and, stirring constantly, cook for about 3–4 minutes over a medium heat.
7 Put in a serving dish with the butter on top. Serve with Polenta Bread (see page 108).

Spinach Toran
(Palak Toran)

Serves 2

450 g (1 lb) fresh spinach
4 tbsp oil
1 small onion, finely chopped
1 green chilli, chopped
75 g (3 oz) tomatoes, peeled and chopped
75 g (3 oz) grated or desiccated coconut
salt

1 Wash the spinach, discard any discoloured leaves and tough stalks, and shake dry. Chop as finely as possible and leave in a colander to drain.
2 Heat the oil in a saucepan and gently fry the onion and green chilli until the onion is transparent.
3 Add the spinach and tomato, cover tightly and cook on a low heat for 4–5 minutes, shaking the saucepan occasionally, until the spinach has collapsed.
4 Stir in the coconut and add salt to taste.

Peas and Cauliflower with Ginger
(Mater Gobi)

Serves 2

3 tbsp oil
25 g (1 oz) ginger, cut into very thin strips
1 small cauliflower, broken into large florets
225 g (8 oz) peas
1 tsp ground turmeric
1 tsp salt
2 tbsp coriander leaves, chopped

1 Heat the oil in a karai or saucepan over a medium high heat. Add the ginger and fry, stirring constantly, until slightly browned.
2 Add the cauliflower, peas, turmeric and salt and mix with the ginger.
3 Lower the heat, cover and, stirring occasionally, cook for about 20–25 minutes until the vegetables are tender.
4 Garnish with the coriander leaves.

Spinach with Pulses and Vegetables
(Sai Bhaji)

Serves 2

50 g (2 oz) channa dal, washed
600 ml (1 pt) water
3 tbsp oil
1 medium onion, finely chopped
1 cm (½) in ginger, grated
2 cloves garlic, crushed
250 g (9 oz) spinach, washed and chopped
1 medium potato, diced into 1 cm (½ in) cubes
3 tomatoes, chopped
50 g (2 oz) peas
½ tsp ground turmeric
½ tsp chilli powder
1 tsp ground coriander
½ tsp salt

1 Bring the dal to the boil in the water over high heat. Cover and simmer for about 40 minutes until the dal is tender. Drain and save the liquid; make it up to 350 ml (12 fl oz) with water, if necessary.
2 Heat the oil in a large saucepan over medium high heat and fry the onion, ginger and garlic until soft.
3 Add the cooked dal and the rest of the ingredients and stir-fry for 2–3 minutes. Add the liquid, cover, lower the heat to medium low and cook for about 30 minutes.

Spinach with Paneer
(Saag Paneer)

Serves 2

4 tbsp oil

175 g (6 oz) paneer (see page 15), drained and
    cut into 1 cm (½ in) cubes

1 large onion, finely sliced

4 cloves garlic, crushed

1 cm (½ in) ginger, grated

350 g (12 oz) frozen spinach, chopped

½ tsp ground turmeric

¾ tsp chilli powder

1 tsp ground coriander

¾ tsp salt

1 Heat the oil in a karai over medium high heat and
   fry the paneer until brown. Set aside.

2 Add the onion, garlic and ginger to the remaining
   oil and fry until golden.

3 Add the spinach, turmeric, chilli, coriander and
   salt and fry for 2–3 minutes.

4 Lower the heat to medium, cover and cook
   a further 10 minutes.

5 Add the fried paneer and, stirring constantly, cook
   until dry.

Cabbage with Peas
(Bund Gobi Aur Mater)

Serves 4
3 tbsp oil
2 bay leaves
¾ tsp whole cumin seeds
700 g (1½ lb) cabbage, finely shredded
1 tsp ground turmeric
1 tsp chilli powder
1½ tsp ground cumin
1 tsp ground coriander
2 tomatoes, chopped
¾ tsp salt
½ tsp sugar
100 g (4 oz) peas

1   Heat the oil in a karai over medium high heat and add the bay leaves and the cumin seeds. Let them sizzle for a few seconds.
2   Add the cabbage and stir for 2–3 minutes.
3   Add the turmeric, chilli, cumin, coriander, tomatoes, salt and sugar and mix with the cabbage.
4   Lower the heat, cover and cook for 15 minutes. Add the peas and cover again. Continue to cook for a further 15 minutes, stirring occasionally.
5   Remove the cover, turn the heat up to medium high and, stirring continuously, cook until dry.

Paneer with Peas
(Mater Paneer)

Serves 4
6 tbsp oil
275 g (10 oz) paneer (see page 15), drained and cut into 1 cm (½ in) pieces
6 tbsp Onion Mix (see page 17)
1 tsp ground turmeric
½ tsp chilli powder
1 tsp ground coriander
¾ tsp salt
175 g (6 oz) peas
250 ml (8 fl oz) water
1 tbsp coriander leaves, chopped (optional)

1   Heat the oil in a karai over medium high heat and fry the paneer pieces until golden brown. Remove and drain on paper towels.
2   In the remaining oil add the onion mixture and fry for 3 minutes, stirring constantly. Add the turmeric, chilli, coriander and salt and continue to fry for a further 2–3 minutes.
3   Add the peas and mix thoroughly. Add the water and bring to the boil. Cover, lower heat to medium low and simmer for 5 minutes. Gently add the pieces of fried paneer and simmer a further 10 minutes. Garnish with the coriander leaves and serve hot.

Dry Peas
(Sukka Mater)

Serves 4

2 tbsp oil

5 cm (2 in) ginger, cut into very thin strips

700 g (1½ lb) peas (fresh or frozen)

1 tsp salt

½ tsp mango powder (amchur)

1. Heat the oil in a karai or saucepan over a medium high heat and fry the ginger, stirring constantly, until slightly browned.
2. Add the peas and salt and mix with the ginger.
3. Lower the heat, cover and cook for about 15 minutes until the peas are tender.
4. Add the mango powder, mix and remove from the heat.

Cabbage with Coconut
(Bund Gobi Aur Narial)

Serves 4

2 tbsp oil
2 bay leaves
¾ tsp whole cumin seeds
1–2 green chillies, chopped
700 g (1½ lb) cabbage, shredded
¾ tsp salt
⅓ tsp sugar
3 tbsp desiccated coconut
½ tsp ground cumin

1   Heat the oil in a karai over medium high heat and add the bay leaves, cumin seeds and the green chillies and let them sizzle for a few seconds.

2   Add the cabbage, salt and sugar and mix. Cover, lower the heat to medium and cook for about 15 minutes until half-done.

3   Add the coconut and ground cumin and fry, stirring constantly for 10–15 minutes until all the moisture has evaporated.

Dry Potatoes
(Sukha Aloo)

Serves 2–3

700 g (1½ lb) potatoes, washed
4 tbsp oil
1 tsp cumin seeds
pinch of asafoetida
¾ tsp ground turmeric
¾ tsp chilli powder
1 tsp ground coriander
1 tsp mango powder (amchur)
1 tsp salt

1 Boil the potatoes with the skins still on. Peel and cut into large pieces (do not overcook them).
2 Heat the oil in a karai or saucepan over a medium high heat. Add the cumin seeds and asafoetida and let them sizzle for about 5–6 seconds.
3 Add the turmeric, chilli, coriander, mango powder and salt and fry for 5–7 seconds. If it starts to stick, sprinkle a little water on the mixture.
4 Add the potatoes and, stirring gently, fry for 5 minutes.

Spicy Potatoes
(Rasadar Aloo)

Serves 2–3

700 g (1½ lb) small potatoes
2–3 medium tomatoes
4 tbsp oil
1 tsp cumin seeds
pinch of asafoetida
¾ tsp ground turmeric
1 tsp ground coriander
¾ tsp chilli powder
1 tsp paprika
1 tsp salt
300 ml (½ pt) water
½ tsp garam masala
2 tbsp coriander leaves, chopped

1 Peel the potatoes and wash them.
2 Place the tomatoes in boiling water for 10 seconds. Carefully peel and chop them.
3 Heat the oil over a medium high heat in a karai or saucepan. Add the cumin seeds and asafoetida and let them sizzle for 5–6 seconds.
4 Add the chopped tomatoes, turmeric, coriander, chilli, paprika and salt and, stirring constantly, fry for 30 seconds. (If it starts to stick to the bottom, sprinkle on a little water.)
5 Add the potatoes and fry for 2–3 minutes, stirring constantly.
6 Add the water and bring to the boil. Lower the heat, cover and cook for about 15 minutes until the potatoes are tender.
7 Add the garam masala and mix.
8 Remove and garnish with the coriander leaves.

Cauliflower with Potato and Tomatoes
(Aloo Gobi Tamatar Masala)

Serves 4

75 g (3 oz) potato
450 g (1 lb) cauliflower
50 g (2 oz) butter or ghee
1 small onion, finely chopped
15 g (½ oz) fresh ginger, finely grated
1 clove garlic, finely chopped
2 green chillies, cut into 4–6 pieces
leaves from 1 sprig of coriander
100 g (4 oz) tomatoes, peeled and
   roughly chopped
½ tsp chilli powder
½ tsp turmeric
½ tsp ground coriander
½ tsp fennel seeds
½ tsp garam masala
1 tsp ground cumin salt

1 Peel the potato and cut into chunks. Divide the cauliflower into florets, discarding the tough stalks. Put the vegetables in a saucepan of cold water to prevent discolouration.

2 Heat three-quarters of the butter or ghee in a heavy-based saucepan and add the onion, ginger, garlic, green chilli and half the coriander leaves. Stir and fry until the onion is golden.

3 Stir in the tomato, add the chilli powder, turmeric, coriander, fennel seeds, garam masala and half the cumin and cook over a low heat, squashing the tomato under the back of a wooden spoon to make a thick paste.

4 Drain and add the vegetables with about 4 tbsp water. Cover and cook for 15 minutes, until the potato is tender but not soft.

5 Meanwhile, heat the remaining butter or ghee in a separate saucepan and add the remaining cumin. Add to the curry with the remaining coriander leaves and salt to taste.

Cauliflower with Coconut and Spices (Narial Phul Gobi Masala)

Serves 4
75 g (3 oz) potato
450 g (1 lb) cauliflower
100 g (4 oz) grated coconut
1 green chilli
15 g (½ oz) fresh ginger, finely grated
1 clove garlic, finely chopped
leaves from 1 sprig of coriander
½ tsp turmeric
1 small onion, finely chopped
4 cashew nuts
2 tbsp oil
1 tsp mustard seeds
4–6 curry leaves
1 red chilli, cut into 4 pieces
75 g (3 oz) tomatoes, chopped
2 tsp lemon juice
salt

1 Peel the potato and cut into chunks. Divide the cauliflower into florets, discarding the tough stalks. Put the vegetables in a saucepan of cold water to prevent discolouration.
2 In a liquidiser, coarsely blend the coconut, green chilli, ginger, garlic, coriander leaves, turmeric, onion and cashew nuts.
3 Drain the vegetables, turn them in the spice mixture to coat and leave for about 10 minutes to absorb the flavours.
4 Heat the oil in a saucepan and when hot, add the mustard seeds, half the curry leaves and the red chilli. Leave them to sizzle for a few seconds until all the seeds have popped.
5 Add the spiced vegetables and tomatoes to the pan, cover and cook on a low heat, stirring occasionally, for about 10 minutes, until the potato is tender but not soft.
6 Sprinkle over the lemon juice, stir in the remaining curry leaves and add salt to taste.

Green Beans and Potato Toran (Aloo Han Moong Toran)

Serves 2
50–75 g (2–3 oz) butter or ghee
1 small onion, finely chopped
225 g (8 oz) tomatoes, peeled and finely chopped
½ tsp garam masala
½ tsp turmeric
½ tsp chilli powder
225 g (8 oz) green beans, trimmed and cut into 2.5 cm (1 in) lengths
225 g (8 oz) potatoes, peeled and diced
1 green chilli, cut into pieces
15 g (½ oz) fresh ginger, finely grated
1 clove garlic, finely chopped
leaves from 1 sprig of coriander
salt

1 Heat the butter or ghee in a large saucepan and fry the onion until golden.
2 Add the tomato, stir well and squash it with the back of a wooden spoon until it forms a paste.
3 Add the garam masala, turmeric and chilli powder and continue to fry, stirring, for about 5 minutes.
4 Add the beans, potatoes, green chilli, ginger, garlic and coriander leaves with 1 tbsp water and cook gently over a low heat, with the lid tightly on, stirring occasionally, for 10–15 minutes, until the vegetables are done. Add salt to taste.

Mushroom with Potatoes and Onions
(Khumbi, Aloo Aur Pyaz)

Serves 2

5 tbsp oil
1 large potato, diced into 2 cm (¾ in) pieces
4 green cardamom pods
4 cm (1½ in) cinnamon stick
2 bay leaves
1 large onion, finely sliced
2 cloves garlic, crushed
2 cm (¾ in) ginger, grated
1 tsp ground turmeric
½ tsp chilli powder
½ tsp salt
a big pinch of sugar
1½ tsp white vinegar
225 g (8 oz) mushrooms, quartered

1 Heat the oil in a karai over medium high heat. Add the potatoes and fry for 2–3 minutes until light golden in colour. Remove the potatoes and set aside.

2 To the same oil add the cardamom pods, cinnamon and bay leaves and let them sizzle for a few seconds.

3 Add the onions, garlic and ginger and fry for 4–5 minutes until soft and golden.

4 Add the turmeric, chilli, salt, sugar and vinegar and fry, stirring continuously, for another minute.

5 Add the mushrooms and potatoes to the spice mixture and mix thoroughly.

6 Lower the heat to medium, cover and cook for about 15 minutes until the potatoes are tender.

Roasted Cauliflower
(Baked Gobi)

Serves 2
4 medium tomatoes
1 large onion
3 cloves garlic
1 cm (½ in) ginger
2 tbsp ghee (see page 16)
¾ tsp ground turmeric
½ tsp chilli powder
½ tsp garam masala (see page 17)
175 g (6 oz) peas
½ tsp salt
1 medium-sized cauliflower, blanched

1 Blend the tomatoes, onion, garlic and ginger in a blender until you have a paste.
2 Heat the ghee in a frying pan over medium heat and add the paste, turmeric, chilli and garam masala and stir-fry until the ghee and spices separate, about 5–6 minutes.
3 Add the peas and salt and cook a further 5 minutes, stirring constantly. Remove from the heat.
4 Chop the cauliflower and place in a large ovenproof dish and pour the spices over it. Place in a preheated oven at 190°C/375°F/Gas Mark 5 for 30–35 minutes. Serve on a flat plate with the peas and spices poured over.

Cauliflower with Coconut Milk
(Narial Phul Gobi)

Serves 4
flesh of 1 coconut, grated
450 g (1 lb) cauliflower, cut into florets, tough stalks discarded
100 g (4 oz) potatoes, peeled and cubed
15 g (½ oz) fresh ginger, finely grated
½ tsp turmeric
½ tsp sambar powder (see page 11)
1 small onion, finely chopped
1 green chilli, sliced
4–6 curry leaves
2–3 tbsp oil
1 tsp mustard seeds
salt
leaves from 1 sprig of coriander

1 Blend the coconut in a liquidiser with 1 tbsp boiling water. Transfer to a sheet of muslin and squeeze the milk into a bowl. Return the coconut to the liquidiser and repeat the process.
2 Simmer the cauliflower and potato in the coconut milk with the ginger, turmeric, sambar powder, three-quarters of the onion and the chilli for about 12 minutes, until the vegetables are tender but not soft. Add the curry leaves.
3 Meanwhile, heat the oil in a saucepan and when hot, add the mustard seeds. Let them sizzle for a few seconds until they have all popped.
4 Add the remaining onion and fry until golden, then add to the curry.
5 Add salt to taste and garnish with coriander.

Cauliflower and Potato Curry
(Aloo Gobi Dalna)

Serves 4

6 tbsp oil
450 g (1 lb) potatoes, peeled and quartered
1 small cauliflower, cut into large florets
pinch of asafoetida
¾ tsp ground turmeric
½ tsp chilli powder
1½ tsp ground cumin
¾ tsp salt
big pinch of sugar
2 tomatoes, chopped
300 ml (1 pt) water
2 tsp ghee (see page 16)
½ tsp garam masala (see page 17)

1 Heat the oil in a karai over medium high heat.
2 Fry the potatoes a few pieces at a time until slightly brown. Remove and set aside.
3 Fry the cauliflower pieces a few at a time until brown spots appear on them. Remove and set aside.
4 Lower the heat to medium, add the asafoetida and after 3–4 seconds add the turmeric, chilli, cumin, salt and sugar. Mix the spices together, add the tomatoes and fry for 1 minute with the spices.
5 Add the water and bring to the boil. Put in the potatoes, cover and cook for 10 minutes.
6 Add the cauliflower, cover again and cook a further 5–7 minutes until the potatoes and cauliflower are tender.
7 Add the ghee and sprinkle with the garam masala and chopped fresh corriander. Remove from the heat and serve hot with rice and red lentils.

Meat and Vegetable Curry
(Sabzi Gosht)

Serves 4
75 g (3 oz) butter or ghee
1 small onion, finely chopped
5 g (½ oz) fresh ginger, grated
2 cloves garlic, chopped
½ tsp turmeric
½ tsp chilli powder
½ tsp ground coriander
½ tsp garam masala
½ tsp ground cumin
1 green chilli, chopped
4–6 curry leaves
450 g (1 lb) meat, trimmed and cubed
175 g (6 oz) tomatoes, peeled and chopped
100 g (4 oz) okra, trimmed and cut into
   2 or 3 pieces
100 g (4 oz) carrots, peeled and diced
225 g (8 oz) potatoes, peeled and cubed
175 g (6 oz) aubergine, peeled and cubed
50 g (2 oz) fresh peas
salt

1   Heat the butter or ghee in a pan, add the onion
    and fry until golden.
2   Add the ginger, garlic, turmeric, chilli powder,
    coriander, garam masala, cumin, green chilli and
    curry leaves, stir and fry for a further 5 minutes.
3   Add the meat and fry for 5 minutes, then add
    the tomato, okra, carrot, potato, aubergine and
    peas, pour on 900 ml (1½ pt) water, add ½ tsp
    salt and cook over a low heat for 1 hour, until the
    vegetables and meat are tender and the sauce
    is thick.
4   Add extra salt to taste.

Meat Kebabs
(Seekh Kebabs)

Serves 4
5 g (½ oz) fresh ginger, finely grated
1 green chilli, chopped
salt
½ tsp garam masala
450 g (1 lb) lean minced meat
1 onion, finely chopped
½ tsp chilli powder
½ tsp ground pepper
½ tsp ground cumin
leaves from 1 sprig of coriander
1 egg, beaten
6 tbsp oil

1   Grind, pound or blend in a liquidiser the ginger,
    green chilli, ½ tsp salt and the garam masala with
    1–2 tbsp water to make a paste.
2   In a bowl, mix the spice paste with the meat and
    onion, sprinkle on the chilli powder, pepper, cumin
    and coriander leaves, add the egg and 1–2 tsp oil
    and combine well.
3   Roll the mixture into small sausages and thread
    onto skewers.
4   Grill the kebabs for 20 minutes, basting with a little
    oil, and turning frequently until cooked through.
5   Remove the kebabs from the skewers and
    fry in the remaining oil for about 10 minutes,
    turning gently.

Pork Vindaloo
(Soor Vindaloo)

Serves 4

6 cloves garlic
25 g (1 oz) fresh ginger
4 red chillies, seeded
1 tsp mustard seeds
½ tsp fenugreek seeds
½ tsp turmeric
½ tsp ground cumin
4 tbsp white wine vinegar
2–3 tbsp oil
2 onions, finely chopped
225 g (8 oz) tomatoes, peeled and chopped
1–1.4 kg (2–3 lb) of shoulder of pork, trimmed
   and cubed
salt
600 ml (1 pt) boiling water
4–6 curry leaves
6 cloves
2.5 cm (1 in) cinnamon stick
1 tsp sugar

1 Chop 4 cloves garlic with half the ginger, then grind, pound or blend in a liquidiser with the chillies, mustard seeds, fenugreek seeds, turmeric, cumin and half the vinegar.
2 Heat the oil, add the onion and fry until golden.
3 Add the spice paste, stir and fry gently for 15 minutes.
4 Add the tomato and continue to cook, mashing it under the back of a wooden spoon to make a paste.
5 When the oil has run clear of the spices, add the pork and fry for 5 minutes, turning the pieces in the spice mixture.
6 Add ½ tsp salt and pour on the boiling water. Simmer, covered, for 40 minutes, until the pork is tender.
7 Slice the remaining garlic and ginger and add with the curry leaves, cloves and cinnamon stick. Cook for a further 5 minutes.
8 Add the sugar and remaining vinegar. Add salt to taste.

Chicken Curry with Nuts and Coconut Milk
(Narial Gosht)

Serves 4

flesh of 1 coconut, grated
50 g (2 oz) cashew nuts
2 cloves garlic, chopped
½ tsp chilli powder
5 g (½ oz) fresh ginger, grated
½ tsp ground coriander
½ tsp turmeric
leaves from 1 sprig of coriander
½ tsp garam masala
½ tsp ground pepper
100 g (4 oz) butter or ghee
1 small onion, chopped
1 kg (2 lb 3 oz) chicken, trimmed and cubed
¼ tsp saffron
25 g (1 oz) sultanas
50 g (2 oz) almonds
salt
4–6 curry leaves

1 Blend the coconut in a liquidiser with 1 tbsp boiling water. Transfer to a sheet of muslin and squeeze out the milk into a bowl. Return the coconut to the liquidiser and repeat the process.
2 Grind, pound or blend in a liquidiser the cashew nuts, garlic, chilli powder, ginger, ground coriander, turmeric, coriander leaves, garam masala and pepper.
3 Heat the butter or ghee in a pan, add the onion and fry until golden, then add the blended spices and fry for a further 5 minutes.
4 Add the chicken, stir and fry for 5 minutes, then pour on the coconut milk, add the saffron, sultanas, almonds and ½ tsp salt and cook, covered, over a low heat for about 1 hour, until the chicken is tender and the sauce has thickened.
5 Sprinkle on the curry leaves.

Meatball and Cauliflower Curry
(Phul Gobi Kofta)

Serves 4

1 egg, beaten
450 g (1 lb) lean
  minced meat
15 g (½ oz) fresh
  ginger, grated
2 cloves garlic,
  chopped
½ tsp garam masala
½ tsp ground cumin
leaves from 1 sprig
  of coriander
salt
small cauliflower, cut
  into florets, tough
  stalks discarded

Sauce

75 g (3 oz) butter
  or ghee
1 small onion,
  finely chopped

cardamom seeds from
  2 pods, crushed
2 cloves
2.5 cm (1 in)
  cinnamon stick
5 g (½ oz) fresh
  ginger, grated
2 cloves garlic,
  crushed
½ tsp turmeric
1 tsp chilli powder
½ tsp ground cumin
½ tsp ground
  coriander
225 g (8 oz) tomatoes,
  peeled and
  chopped or 2 tbsp
  tomato purée
150 ml (¼ pt) yoghurt
salt
leaves from 1 sprig
  of coriander

1. Mix the egg with the minced meat.
2. Grind, pound or blend in a liquidiser the ginger, garlic, garam masala, cumin, coriander leaves and ½ tsp salt.
3. Mix the spice paste with the meat, form it into small balls and set aside.
4. To make the sauce, heat the butter or ghee in a pan, add the onion and fry until golden.
5. Add the cardamom seeds, cloves, cinnamon, ginger, garlic, turmeric, chilli powder, cumin and coriander and fry for 3–4 minutes, stirring.
6. Add the tomato or tomato purée and cook, stirring, until the fat runs clear of the spices.
7. Stir in the yoghurt with a pinch of salt and 1–2 tbsp water and bring gently to the boil.
8. Carefully slide in the meatballs and cauliflower florets and cook for about 20 minutes on a low heat, stirring occasionally and taking care not to break the meatballs.
9. Sprinkle on the chopped coriander leaves and add salt to taste.

Sweet and Sour Lamb Curry
(Chuteraney)

Serves 4

2 tbsp oil	½ tsp garam masala
50 g (2 oz) butter or ghee	½ tsp turmeric
	1 tsp chilli powder
2 onions, finely chopped	1 kg (2 lb 3 oz) lamb, trimmed and cubed
1 green chilli, chopped	600 ml (1 pt) boiling water
15 g (1 oz) fresh ginger, finely grated	225 g (8 oz) potatoes, peeled and chopped
2 cloves garlic, crushed	½ tsp ground pepper
225 g (8 oz) tomatoes, peeled and chopped	1 tbsp sugar
	150 ml (¼ pt) yoghurt
leaves from 2 sprigs of coriander	2 tbsp lemon juice
	salt

1 Heat the oil and butter or ghee in a pan, add the onion, green chilli, ginger and garlic and fry until the onion turns golden.

2 Add the tomato, half the coriander leaves, the garam masala, turmeric and chilli powder and cook, stirring and squashing the tomato under the back of a wooden spoon until it makes a paste and the fat has run clear of the spices.

3 Add the lamb and boiling water and cook over a low heat for about 1 hour, until tender.

4 Add the potato and cook for a further 10–15 minutes until tender but not soft.

5 Mix the remaining coriander leaves, the pepper and sugar with the yoghurt, add to the curry and cook for 2–3 minutes, stirring, to heat through.

6 Sprinkle on the lemon juice and chilli powder and add salt to taste.

Lamb Curry with Roast Spices
(Masala Gosht)

Serves 4

3 tbsp oil
2 tbsp coriander seeds
2 red chillies, cut into pieces
2.5 cm (1 in) cinnamon stick
3 cloves
50 g (2 oz) grated coconut
450 g (1 lb) lamb, trimmed and cubed
½ tsp turmeric
salt
2 green chillies, sliced
15 g (½ oz) fresh ginger, grated
1 small onion, chopped
225 g (8 oz) potatoes, peeled and diced
225 g (8 oz) tomatoes, peeled and chopped
900 ml (1½ pt) boiling water
6 mint leaves
flaked almonds (optional garnish)
red chilli (optional garnish)

1 Heat half the oil in a saucepan and fry the coriander seeds, red chilli, cinnamon, cloves and coconut for about 5 minutes, then transfer to a grinder or a mortar and reduce to a smooth paste.

2 Put the lamb in a bowl with the turmeric, ½ tsp salt, green chilli, ginger and half the onion, add the spice paste and mix well. Leave to marinate for 15 minutes.

3 Heat the remaining oil in a large saucepan and fry the remaining onion until golden.

4 Add the marinated lamb, the potato and tomato, pour on the boiling water, cover and cook on a low heat for about 1 hour, until the lamb is tender and the sauce is thick.

5 Add extra salt to taste and sprinkle on the mint leaves, flaked almonds and chopped chilli.

Plain Beef Curry
(Gosht Curry)

Serves 4

1 kg (2 lb 3 oz) beef, trimmed and cubed
600 ml (1 pt) water
1 tbsp lemon juice
salt
2 tbsp ground coriander
2 tsp chilli powder
½ tsp ground pepper
½ tsp ground cumin
½ tsp turmeric
50 g (2 oz) butter or ghee
1 tbsp oil
1 small onion, finely chopped
25 g (1 oz) fresh ginger, chopped
2 cloves garlic, chopped
1 tsp garam masala
4–6 curry leaves

1 Wash the beef thoroughly in hot water. Drain and cook, covered, in the measured amount of water with the lemon juice and a pinch of salt for about an hour or until the beef is tender and most of the liquid has evaporated.
2 Mix the coriander, chilli, pepper, cumin and turmeric with 2 tbsp water to make a smooth paste.
3 Heat the butter or ghee in a saucepan with the oil, add the onion, ginger and garlic and fry until the onion is golden.
4 Add the spice paste and continue to fry for 10 minutes. Add the paste to the cooked beef with ½ tsp salt and cook, covered, on a low heat for 10–15 minutes, until the sauce is thick.
5 Sprinkle on the garam masala and the curry leaves and add extra salt to taste.

Beef and Tomato Curry
(Tamatar Gosht)

Serves 4

50 g (2 oz) butter or ghee
1 small onion, finely chopped
15 g (½ oz) fresh ginger, finely grated
3 cloves garlic, finely chopped
225 g (8 oz) tomatoes, peeled and chopped
½ tsp turmeric
2 tsp chilli powder
1 tbsp ground coriander
½ tsp ground cumin
salt
1 tsp garam masala
600 ml (1 pt) boiling water
1 kg (2 lb 3 oz) beef, trimmed and cubed
225 g (8 oz) potatoes, peeled and diced
leaves from 1 sprig of coriander

1 Heat the butter or ghee in a large saucepan, add the onion, ginger and garlic and fry until the onion is golden.
2 Add the tomato, turmeric, chilli powder, ground coriander, cumin, ½ tsp salt and garam masala. Stir and continue to fry until the fat runs clear of the spices, then add the boiling water and mix well.
3 Add the beef and cook, covered, over a low heat for about 1 hour, until tender and the sauce is thick.
4 Add the potato and a little extra water, if necessary, and cook for a further 10–15 minutes until tender but not soft.
5 Sprinkle on the coriander leaves and extra salt to taste.

Beef Curry in a Thick Sauce
(Gosht Dupiaza)

Serves 4

1 small onion, finely chopped
2 tbsp oil
1 tbsp plain flour
1 kg (2 lb 3 oz) beef, trimmed and cubed
1 tbsp lemon juice
½ tsp ground pepper
salt
900 ml (1½ pt) water
50 g (2 oz) butter or ghee
225 g (8 oz) tomatoes, chopped
1 green chilli, sliced
leaves from 1 sprig of coriander
½ tsp garam masala

1 Fry the onion in the oil until golden. Add the flour and continue to fry, stirring, until the flour is coloured and has formed a paste.

2 Add the beef, lemon juice, pepper and ½ tsp salt, stir and pour on the water. Bring to the boil and simmer, covered, for about 1 hour, stirring occasionally, until the meat is tender and the sauce is thick.

3 Heat the butter or ghee in a pan, add the tomato and green chilli and fry gently, stirring, for 3–4 minutes, then add to the meat.

4 Sprinkle on the coriander leaves and garam masala.

Meat Curry with Yoghurt
(Dahi Gosht)

Serves 4

4–6 tbsp oil
2 onions, roughly chopped
25 g (1 oz) fresh ginger, chopped
2 cloves garlic, chopped
1 green chilli, chopped
cardamom seeds from 2 pods
2.5 cm (1 in) cinnamon stick
3 cloves
½ tsp fennel seeds
1 tbsp ground coriander
1 tsp ground cumin
leaves from 2 sprigs coriander
½ tsp turmeric
1 tsp chilli powder
150 ml (¼ pt) yoghurt
1 kg (2 lb 3 oz) meat, trimmed and cubed
600 ml (1 pt) boiling water
4–6 curry leaves
salt

1 Heat half the oil in a pan, add half the onion, the ginger, garlic, green chilli, cardamom seeds, cinnamon, cloves, fennel seeds, ground coriander, cumin, half the coriander leaves, the turmeric and chilli and fry gently, stirring, for 10 minutes.

2 Take the saucepan off the heat and stir in the yoghurt. Mix well and set aside.

3 Chop the remaining onion finely and fry in the remaining oil until golden. Add the cubed meat and fry for about 15 minutes, stirring occasionally.

4 Stir in the spiced yoghurt and cook gently for 8–10 minutes, stirring.

5 Pour on the boiling water, turn down the heat and cook, covered, for about 1 hour or until the meat is tender. Cook uncovered if a thicker sauce is required and stir frequently.

6 Sprinkle on the curry leaves and remaining coriander leaves and add salt to taste.

Fried Spiced Beef Keema
(Keema Masala)

Serves 4

100 g (4 oz) butter or ghee
1 onion, finely chopped
2 cloves garlic, finely chopped
15 g (½ oz) fresh ginger, finely grated
leaves from 1 sprig of coriander
75 g (6 oz) tomatoes, peeled and chopped
cardamom seeds from 2 pods, crushed
2.5 cm (1 in) cinnamon stick
3 cloves
1 bay leaf
½ tsp ground coriander
½ tsp turmeric
½ tsp ground cumin
½ tsp chilli powder
salt
1 kg (2 lb 3 oz) beef
225 g (8 oz) potatoes, peeled and diced
300 ml (½ pt) boiling water
50 g (2 oz) peas (fresh or frozen)

1 Heat the butter or ghee in a pan, add the onion and fry until golden.

2 Add the garlic, ginger, half the coriander leaves, the tomato, cardamom, cinnamon, cloves and bay leaf and fry for 3–4 minutes, stirring.

3 Add the coriander, turmeric, cumin, chilli powder and ½ tsp salt and stir to make a thick paste.

4 Add the beef and potato and fry for about 15 minutes, stirring occasionally, then pour on the boiling water, cover and cook on a low heat for 15 minutes, until the beef and potato are cooked and the sauce is thick. Add the peas at the end and cook for a further couple of minutes.

5 Add salt to taste and sprinkle on the remaining coriander leaves.

Lamb with Cardamom
(Elaichi Gosht)

Serves 4–6
30 black peppercorns
cardamom seeds from 25 pods
5 medium tomatoes
2.5 cm (1 in) ginger, cut into small pieces
120 ml (4 fl oz) oil
2 large onions, finely chopped
1 kg (2 lb) lamb, cut into 2.5 cm (1 in) cubes
2 tsp paprika
1½ tsp salt
250 ml (8 fl oz) water
3 tbsp coriander leaves, chopped

1   Grind the peppercorns and cardamom
    seeds finely.
2   In a liquidiser or processor, blend the tomatoes
    and ginger.
3   Heat the oil in a saucepan and fry the onions until
    golden. Add the meat and the ground spices. Stir
    constantly and fry for 5 minutes.
4   Add the blended mixture, paprika and salt, mix
    with the meat and fry for a further 2–3 minutes.
5   Add the water, bring it to the boil, cover, lower the
    heat to very low and cook for about 1 hour until
    tender. Garnish with coriander leaves and serve
    with rice.

Lamb Chop Kebabs
(Bara Kabob)

Serves 4
700 g (1½ lb) lamb chops
475 ml (16 fl oz) yoghurt
1½ tsp salt
2.5 cm (1 in) ginger, grated
8 cloves garlic, crushed
¾ tsp garam masala powder
1 tbsp poppy seeds, ground
2–3 green chillies, ground
2 tbsp oil

1   Remove excess fat from the chops. Wash and
    pat dry.
2   Lightly beat the yoghurt and mix in all
    the ingredients.
3   Add the lamb chops and marinate for at least
    6 hours. It is best to marinate for 24 hours – if you
    are going to marinate for this long, cover and
    refrigerate the meat but make sure it is returned
    to room temperature before it is grilled.
4   Preheat the grill.
5   Take the chops out of the marinade and place
    on a baking sheet. Grill for 8–10 minutes on
    each side.

Chicken, Tandoori Style
(Murghi Tandoori)

Serves 4

8 chicken breast
1–2 tbsp lemon juice
salt
5 g (½ oz) fresh ginger, finely grated
3 cloves garlic, chopped
1 tsp ground coriander
½ tsp ground cumin
1 tsp chilli powder
2 tbsp paprika
red food colouring (optional)
1 tsp garam masala
½ tsp ground black pepper
150 ml (¼ pt) yoghurt
1 cucumber, sliced
1 small onion, sliced

1 Skin the chicken breasts, wash thoroughly and dry on absorbent kitchen paper. Slash them with a sharp pointed knife.
2 Rub in the lemon juice and sprinkle with salt.
3 Blend the ginger and garlic in a liquidiser with 1 tbsp water, then mix with the coriander, cumin, chilli powder, paprika, red food colouring, garam masala and pepper and stir into the yoghurt.
4 Smother the chicken breast in the spiced yoghurt and leave, covered, in the fridge to marinate overnight.
5 Lay the chicken breast on a rack across a roasting tin and cook in the oven at 200°C/400°F/Gas Mark 6 for about 45 minutes, until tender.
6 Sprinkle with extra salt to taste and garnish with cucumber and onion slices.

FISH AND SHELLFISH

There are said to be over 2,000 varieties of fish and shellfish available in India and they form an important part of the diet, especially for non-meat-eaters. The cold-water fish that swim in the seas around Europe and America are not natives to the warm waters of the Indian Ocean, but they are equally well suited to Indian cookery. Best varieties are the firm-fleshed white fish such as cod, haddock or halibut.

Sardines in a Thick Spicy Sauce
(Machli Curry)

Serves 4
3 tbsp oil
2 tbsp coriander seeds
3 red chillies, cut into pieces
50–75 g (2–3 oz) grated coconut
1–2 tbsp tamarind juice
1 green chilli, chopped
15 g (½ oz) fresh ginger, finely grated
1 onion, finely chopped
¼ tsp turmeric
450 g (1 lb) fresh sardines, cleaned
salt
4–6 curry leaves

1 Heat half the oil in a pan, add the coriander seeds and red chilli and fry for 3–4 minutes until the fragrance emerges, then grind, pound or blend with the coconut.
2 Return to the saucepan and continue to fry, adding the tamarind, green chilli, ginger, half the onion and the turmeric, for a further 5–7 minutes, until they make a thick paste.
3 Lay the sardines on a plate, smother them in the paste and leave to marinate for 15 minutes.
4 Meanwhile, heat the remaining oil and fry the remaining onion until golden.
5 Add the marinated sardines to the saucepan with 2 tbsp water, cover and cook on a low heat for 5–8 minutes, until tender.
6 Add salt to taste and sprinkle on the curry leaves.

Fried Spiced Fish
(Machi Masala)

Serves 2
1 onion, finely chopped
5 g (½ oz) fresh ginger, finely grated
6 curry leaves
salt
¼ tsp turmeric
1 tsp chilli powder
4 tbsp oil
450 g (1 lb) white fish, boned, skinned and cubed

1 Pound, grind or blend in a liquidiser the onion, ginger, curry leaves, ½ tsp salt, the turmeric and chilli powder to make a thick paste.
2 Spread the paste over the fish and leave to marinate for about 2 hours.
3 Heat the oil in a large saucepan that the fish will fit into in one layer, add the fish and fry for about 10 minutes, until tender.
4 Add extra salt to taste.

Prawn Biriyani
(Jhinga Biriyani)

Serves 4

Prawns

1 green chilli
15 g (½ oz) fresh
   ginger, grated
1 clove garlic, chopped
50 g (2 oz) grated or
   desiccated coconut
4 cashew nuts
2 tsp biriyani masala
   (see page 8˜)
50 g (2 oz) butter
   or ghee
1 small onion,
   chopped
450 g (1 lb)
   shelled prawns
salt
1 tbsp lemon juice

cashew nuts and
   sultanas, fried in a
   little butter or ghee,
   for decoration

Rice

50 g (2 oz) butter or
   ghee
small onion, chopped
2 bay leaves
225 g (8 oz) basmati
   rice, washed,
   soaked in water
   for 20 minutes
   and drained
salt
100 g (4 oz) fresh peas

1 Grind, pound or blend in a liquidiser the chilli,
   ginger, garlic, coconut, cashews and biriyani
   masala to make a thick paste.
2 Heat the butter or ghee in a pan, add the onion
   and fry until golden.
3 Add the blended spice paste and fry for a further
   5–8 minutes, stirring.
4 Add the prawns and ½ tsp salt and cook on a low
   heat for 3–4 minutes, stirring, until the prawns are
   heated through and coated in the spice mixture.
5 For the rice, heat the butter or ghee in a pan, add
   the onion and bay leaves and fry until the onion
   turns golden.
6 Pour on the rice, stir and fry for about 10 minutes,
   until translucent.
7 Add 1 tsp salt, the peas and enough water to
   cover and simmer on a low heat for
   10–15 minutes, until the rice is almost cooked.
8 Stir the prawns and rice together in an ovenproof
   casserole, cover with a lid or foil and cook in
   the oven at 150°C/300°F/Gas Mark 2 for
   10–15 minutes.
9 Sprinkle over the lemon juice, cashews and
   sultanas and add extra salt to taste.

Prawn Vindaloo
(Jhinga Vindaloo)

Serves 4

½ tsp cumin seeds

25 g (1 oz) fresh
ginger, finely grated

1–2 cloves garlic,
finely chopped

1 tsp mustard seeds

3 tbsp oil

2 onions, finely
chopped

6 curry leaves

100 g (4 oz) tomatoes,
peeled and
chopped

2 tsp chilli powder

½ tsp turmeric

450 g (1 lb) shelled
prawns (or
langoustines)

3 tbsp white wine
vinegar

1 tsp cornflour
(optional)

salt

½ tsp sugar (optional)

1 Crush the cumin seeds with the ginger, garlic and
mustard seeds.

2 Heat the oil in a pan, add the onion and curry
leaves and fry until the onion is golden.

3 Add the tomato, chilli powder, turmeric and
1–2 tbsp water and cook, mashing the tomato
under the back of a wooden spoon to make a
thick paste.

4 Add the crushed spices and continue to fry for
5 minutes, then add the prawns or langoustines
and 4 tbsp water and simmer for 10 minutes.

5 Pour on the vinegar. The sauce may be thickened,
if necessary, by adding the cornflour mixed with
1 tsp water. Add salt to taste and sugar, if liked.

Spiced Prawns
(Jhinga Batana)

Serves 4

450 g (1 lb) prawns
1½ tsp salt
½ tsp ground turmeric
4 cloves garlic
2 cm (¾ in) ginger
2 green chillis
6 tbsp oil
2 medium onions, finely chopped
1½ tsp ground coriander
1½ tsp ground cumin
175 ml (6 fl oz) water
175 g (6 oz) peas
1 tsp treacle or brown sugar
2 tbsp tamarind juice (see page 16)
2 tbsp chopped coriander leaves
2 tbsp grated coconut

1 Shell the prawns, leaving the tails on. Make a small cut along the back to remove the black vein. Wash the prawns and rub in ½ tsp of the salt and turmeric. Put aside for 1 hour.

2 Grind the garlic, ginger and green chillies to a paste.

3 In a large saucepan, heat the oil and fry the onions until lightly golden.

4 Add the prawns and paste and stir-fry for 2–3 minutes.

5 Add the coriander, cumin and remaining salt, and continue to fry for a further minute.

6 Add the water, bring to the boil, reduce the heat to medium low, cover and simmer for 10 minutes.

7 Add the peas, treacle or sugar and tamarind juice, cover again and cook for about 20 minutes until the prawns are tender. Garnish with the coriander leaves and coconut.

Fish Cooked in Coconut Milk
(Mouli)

Serves 4

700 g (1½ lb) white fish, cleaned
50 g (2 oz) creamed coconut
250 ml (8 fl oz) boiling water
4 tbsp oil
3 cloves
1 medium onion, finely chopped
¼ tsp ground turmeric
1 tsp salt
3–4 green chillies
6–8 curry leaves

1 Cut the fish into 8–10 equal-sized pieces.
2 Blend together the creamed coconut and the boiling water in a blender or food processor until smooth.
3 Heat the oil over a medium heat and fry the pieces of fish, a few at a time, until lightly browned. Keep on one side.
4 Add the cloves to the remaining oil. When they swell up, add the onion and fry until lightly golden. Add the turmeric and salt and stir-fry for a few seconds.
5 Add the fish gently and mix.
6 Add the coconut milk and, when it starts to boil, cover, lower the heat to medium low and cook for about 10–12 minutes.
7 Add the chillies and curry leaves and cook for a further couple of minutes until the fish is tender. Serve hot with rice.

Fish in a Yoghurt Sauce
(Dahi Mach)

Serves 4

1½ tsp salt
700 g (1½ lb) white fish, cleaned and cut into 2.5 cm (1 in) pieces
4 tbsp ghee (see page 16)
6 green cardamom pods
5 cm (2 in) cinnamon stick
2 bay leaves
1 medium onion, finely sliced
2 cm (¾ in) ginger, grated
1 tbsp raisins
2–3 green chillies
about 120 ml (4 fl oz) natural yoghurt
175 ml (6 fl oz) water
½ tsp sugar

1 Sprinkle ½ tsp of salt on the fish and rub into the pieces.
2 Heat the ghee in a karai or saucepan over a medium high heat, and gently fry the pieces of fish, a few at a time, until lightly golden. Put aside.
3 In the remaining ghee, add the cardamom, cinnamon and bay leaves and let them sizzle for 3–4 seconds.
4 Add the onion, ginger and raisins and fry, stirring constantly, until the onion is golden.
5 Add the chillies, yoghurt and water, sugar and the remaining salt and bring to the boil. Gently add the pieces of fish. Cover, lower the heat and cook for 15–20 minutes until the fish is cooked and the gravy slightly thickened.

Prawns in a Coconut Sauce
(Chingre Macher Malai)

Serves 4

450 g (1 lb) prawns
1½ tsp ground turmeric
1½ tsp salt
50 g (2 oz) creamed coconut
300 ml (½ pt) hot water
120 ml (4 fl oz) oil
2 medium potatoes, peeled and quartered
1 large onion, finely sliced
½ tsp chilli powder
½ tsp sugar
2–3 green chillies

1 Shell the prawns, leaving the tails on. Make a small cut along the back to remove the black vein. Wash and pat dry. Rub ½ tsp each of turmeric and salt into the prawns.
2 In a food processor or liquidiser, blend together the creamed coconut and water. Put aside.
3 Heat the oil in a saucepan and fry the potatoes until evenly browned. Put aside.
4 Add the prawns and fry until golden. Put aside.
5 Add the onion to the remaining oil and fry until golden brown. Add the remaining turmeric, salt, chilli powder and sugar and fry for 1–2 minutes with the onion.
6 Add the blended coconut milk and bring to the boil. Add the prawns and green chillies.
7 Cover, lower the heat and cook for 10 minutes. Add the potatoes, cover again and cook for a further 20–25 minutes, until the prawns are cooked and the gravy thickened.

Fish Curry
(Macher Kalia)

Serves 4

700 g (1½ lb) white fish, cleaned
1½ tsp ground turmeric
1½ tsp salt
1 medium onion, quartered
2 cloves garlic
2 cm (¾ in) ginger
1 tbsp vinegar
8 tbsp oil
2 medium potatoes, peeled and quartered
4 green cardamom pods
5 cm (2 in) cinnamon stick, broken in half
2 bay leaves
½ tsp chilli powder
¼ tsp sugar
300 ml (½ pt) water
3–4 green chillies

1 Cut the fish into 8–10 equal-sized pieces.
2 Rub ½ tsp each of turmeric and salt into the fish.
3 In a food processor or liquidiser, blend together the onion, garlic, ginger and vinegar.
4 Heat the oil in a karai or saucepan and fry the potatoes, turning often, until evenly browned. Put aside.
5 Gently add a few pieces of fish and fry until golden. Put aside.
6 In the remaining oil, add the cardamom, cinnamon and bay leaves and let them sizzle for 5–6 seconds.
7 Add the blended mixture and, stirring constantly, fry until golden brown.
8 Add the remaining turmeric, salt, chilli powder and sugar, mix thoroughly with the onion mixture and fry for 1–2 minutes.
9 Add the water and green chillies and bring to the boil. Add the pieces of potato and fish. Cover, lower the heat and cook for 15–20 minutes until the potatoes are tender. Serve with rice.

Fish in a Hot Sauce
(Macher Jhal)

Serves 4

700 g (1½ lb) white fish, cleaned
1½ tsp ground turmeric
1½ tsp salt
120 ml (4 fl oz) oil
1 large onion, finely sliced
½ tsp chilli powder
250 ml (4 fl oz) water
2–3 green chillies

1 Cut the fish into 8–10 equal-sized pieces.
2 Rub ½ tsp each of turmeric and salt into the fish.
3 Heat the oil in a karai or saucepan over a medium high heat and fry the pieces of fish, a few at a time, until lightly browned. Put aside.
4 In the remaining oil, fry the onion until brown. Add the remaining turmeric, salt and chilli powder and stir-fry for a further 1 minute.
5 Add the water and bring to the boil; gently add the pieces of fish and the green chillies. Cover, lower the heat to medium and cook for about 15 minutes until the fish is cooked and the gravy thickened.

Steamed Prawns
(Bhape Chirigre)

Serves 2

450 g (1 lb) prawns
1 tsp ground turmeric
½ tsp chilli powder
1 tsp black mustard seeds, ground
2–3 green chillies
1 tsp salt
2 tbsp oil

1. Shell the prawns, leaving the tails on. Make a small cut down the back to remove the black vein. Wash and pat dry.
2. Thoroughly mix all the ingredients with the prawns. Place the mixture in a bowl (half-fill it only), and tie a double thickness of aluminium foil around the top of the bowl.
3. In a large saucepan, boil some water and place the bowl of prawns in the saucepan, so that the water reaches a quarter of the way up the bowl.
4. Cover the saucepan, lower the heat and keep boiling, topping up the boiling water during cooking as necessary. Steam for about 30–40 minutes.

Leavened Bread
(Naan)

1 tsp dried yeast
1 tsp sugar
75 ml (3 fl oz) lukewarm water
275 g (10 oz) plain flour
½ tsp salt
¾ tsp baking powder
1 tbsp oil
about 3 tbsp plain yoghurt

1 Stir the yeast and sugar into the water and set aside for 15–20 minutes until the liquid is frothy.
2 Sieve together the flour, salt and baking powder. Make a well in the middle, add the yeast liquid, oil and yoghurt and knead for about 10 minutes until soft and no longer sticky.
3 Place the dough in an oiled plastic bag and set aside in a warm place for 2–3 hours until double in size.
4 Preheat the oven to 200°C/400°F/Gas Mark 6. Knead the dough again for 1–2 minutes and divide into 12 balls. Roll into 18 cm (7 in) rounds.
5 Place as many as possible on a baking sheet and put in the oven for around 4–5 minutes each side, until brown spots appear. Place them under a hot grill for a few seconds until slightly browned.
6 Wrap the cooked ones in foil while cooking the others.

Yoghurt Bread
(Batora)

225 g (8 oz) plain flour
1½ tsp baking powder
½ tsp salt
1 tsp sugar
1 egg, beaten
about 3 tbsp yoghurt
oil for deep frying

1 Sieve the flour, baking powder and salt together. Mix in the sugar.
2 Add the beaten egg and enough yoghurt to form a stiff dough. Knead for 10–15 minutes until you have a soft, smooth dough. Cover with a cloth and let it rest for 3–4 hours.
3 Knead again on a floured surface for 5 minutes. Divide into 12–14 balls.
4 Roll out on a floured surface into 12.5 cm (5 in) rounds.
5 Heat the oil in a karai over high heat. Fry the batoras, pressing in the middle with a slotted spoon so that they puff up. Turn and cook the other side for a few seconds until lightly browned. Drain. Serve hot with Spiced Chickpeas or Soured Chickpeas (see pages 38-39).

Stuffed Deep-fried Bread
(Mater Kachori)

Filling
1 tbsp ghee (see page 16)
pinch of asafoetida
5 mm (¾ in) fresh ginger, grated
225 g (8 oz) peas, boiled and mashed
¼ tsp chilli powder
¼ tsp salt
½ tsp garam masala (see page 17)

Dough
225 g (8 oz) plain flour
½ tsp salt
1½ tsp ghee
approx 120 ml (4 fl oz) hot water
oil for deep frying

1 To make the filling, heat the ghee in a karai over medium heat, add the asafoetida and ginger and fry for a few seconds.
2 Add the mashed peas, chilli and salt and, stirring constantly, fry for about 5 minutes until the mixture leaves the sides and forms a ball. Mix in the garam masala and set aside to cool.
3 To make the dough, sieve the flour and salt together. Rub in the ghee. Add enough water to make a stiff dough. Knead for about 10 minutes to form a soft pliable dough. Divide into 20 balls.
4 Insert your thumb into the middle of each ball to form a cup. Fill with 1 tsp of the filling. Seal the top and make it into a ball again.
5 Flatten and roll into 10 cm (4 in) rounds on a slightly oiled surface (take care that no holes appear when rolling).
6 Heat the oil in a karai until very hot. Gently put in a kachori and press the middle so that it puffs up. Turn and fry the other side until lightly golden. Drain on kitchen paper and serve hot with Potato Masala Curry (see page 58).

Deep-fried Brown Bread
(Poori)

225 g (8 oz) wholewheat flour
½ tsp salt
2 tbsp oil
about 90 ml (3½ oz) hot water
oil for deep frying

1 Sieve together the flour and salt. Rub in the oil. Add enough water to make a stiff dough.
2 Put the dough on a floured surface and knead for about 10 minutes till soft and smooth.
3 Divide the mixture into 20 balls.
4 Taking one ball at a time, flatten them on a slightly oiled surface and roll into rounds of 10 cm (4 in) across. (Do not stack the rolled pooris on one another as they might stick together.)
5 Heat the oil in a karai until very hot and add a poori, pressing the middle with a slotted spoon so that it puffs up. Quickly turn and cook the other side for a few seconds. Drain and serve hot.

Rice with Pulses
(Khichuri)

Serves 4

75 g (3 oz) moong dal
75 g (3 oz) red lentils, washed
6 tbsp oil
2 bay leaves
5 cm (2 in) cinnamon stick
4 green cardamom pods
3 cloves garlic, crushed
2.5 cm (1 in) fresh ginger, grated
1 large onion, finely sliced
1 tsp ground turmeric
½ tsp chilli powder
1 tsp salt
⅓ tsp sugar
1 tomato, chopped
75 g (3 oz) basmati rice, washed and drained
1.25 l (2¼ pt) water
3–4 green chillies, halved lengthways

1 In a small saucepan dry roast the moong dal over medium heat, until it turns light brown. Remove from the heat, wash thoroughly, and mix with the red lentils. Put in a sieve to drain.

2 Heat the oil in a large saucepan over medium heat. Add the bay leaves, cinnamon stick and cardamom pods and let them sizzle for a few seconds.

3 Add the garlic, ginger and onion and fry until the onion is golden brown.

4 Add the turmeric, chilli, salt, sugar and tomato and mix thoroughly. Add the rice and the pulses and continue to fry for 5–7 minutes.

5 Add the water, and when it starts to boil, lower the heat and simmer for about 35–40 minutes.

6 Just before removing from the heat, add the chillies. Serve with ghee (see page 16) and Pakoras (see page 135).

Simple Rice with Pulses
(Khichuri)

Serves 3–4

225 g (8 oz) basmati rice, washed and drained
50 g (2 oz) moong dal, washed and drained
750 ml (1¼ pt) water
1½ tbsp ghee (see page 16)

1 Mix the rice and dal and soak in plenty of water for 1 hour. Drain.
2 Add the rice and dal mixture to the measured water in a large saucepan and bring to the boil over a high heat. Turn the heat down to very low, cover and cook for about 20 minutes until all the water has been absorbed. Remove from the heat.
3 In a small pan, heat the ghee until very hot and pour it over the cooked rice and dal. Mix. Serve hot with Spinach with Pulses and Vegetables (see page 48), yoghurt and poppadoms.

Potato Pillau
(Aloo Pillau)

Serves 4–6

75 g (3 oz) creamed coconut
600 ml (1 pt) hot water
handful coriander leaves
1 tbsp grated coconut
2 green chillies
2 tbsp lemon juice
½ tsp sugar
1½ tsp salt
½ tsp garam masala (see page 17)
¼ tsp ground turmeric
10–12 small new potatoes, washed and peeled
3 tbsp oil
2 cloves
1 medium onion, finely sliced
1 clove garlic, crushed
275 g (10 oz) basmati rice, washed and drained

1 Make the coconut milk by blending together the creamed coconut and hot water. Put aside.
2 Chop the coriander leaves and throw away the lower stalks and roots. Wash them thoroughly.
3 Blend together the coriander leaves, grated coconut, chillies, lemon juice, sugar, ½ tsp salt, garam masala and turmeric until you have a fine paste.
4 Parboil the potatoes. Drain and cool.
5 Take a potato and make two cuts like a cross coming about three-quarters of the way down the length. Take care not to cut right through. Cut all the potatoes in this way.
6 Fill each potato with a little of the coriander paste. If you have any paste left, rub it onto the potatoes.
7 Heat the oil over a medium high heat in a large saucepan. Add the cloves and, after 3–4 seconds, add the onion and garlic and fry until the onion is lightly golden.
8 Add the rice and sauté for 2–3 minutes, stirring constantly.
9 Add the coconut milk and 1 tsp salt and bring to the boil. Add the potatoes, and when it comes to the boil again, lower the heat to very low, cover and cook for about 20 minutes until all the water has been absorbed.
10 Fluff the rice with a fork before serving.

Pea Pillau
(Mater Pillau)

Serves 4–6
3 tbsp oil
½ tsp whole cumin seeds
1 medium onion, finely chopped
100 g (4 oz) peas
350 g (12 oz) basmati rice, washed and drained
1 tsp salt
900 ml (1½ pt) water

1 Heat the oil in a large saucepan over medium heat, add the cumin seeds and let them sizzle for a few seconds.
2 Add the onion and fry until soft. Add the peas, rice and salt and stir-fry for about 5 minutes. Add the water and bring to the boil.
3 Cover tightly, lower the heat to very low and cook for about 20 minutes until all the water has been absorbed. Fluff the pillau with a fork and serve hot.

Vegetable Pillau
(Sabzi Ka Pillau)

Serves 4–6

275 g (10 oz) basmati rice
5 tbsp ghee (see page 16)
2 tbsp unsalted cashew nuts
1 medium onion, finely chopped
1 cm (½ in) ginger, cut into very thin strips
225 (8 oz) French beans, cut into
    4 cm (1½ in) lengths
2 small carrots, peeled and diced
75 g (3 oz) peas
1 small red pepper, seeded and thinly sliced
900 ml (1½ pt) water
1½ tsp salt
1 tbsp coriander leaves

1   Wash the rice in several changes of water and leave in a sieve to drain thoroughly.
2   Heat the ghee in a large saucepan and fry the cashew nuts until golden. Drain and put aside.
3   In the remaining ghee, add the onion and ginger and fry until the onion is soft and transparent.
4   Add the rice and stir-fry for 1–2 minutes. Add all the vegetables and mix with the onion and rice.
5   Add the water and salt and bring to the boil. Give it a good stir, lower the heat to very low, cover and cook for about 20 minutes until the rice and vegetables are tender and all the water is absorbed.
6   Garnish with the fried cashew nuts and coriander leaves.

Pillau with Coconut and Milk
(Narial Aur Dudh Pillau)

Serves 4

350 g (12 oz) basmati rice, rinsed and drained
2 tbsp desiccated coconut
2–3 green chillies
1 tsp salt
½ tsp sugar
2 tbsp raisins
1 tbsp pistachio nuts, skinned and
    cut into thin strips
2 bay leaves
5 cm (2 in) cinnamon stick
4 green cardamom pods
3 tbsp ghee (see page 16)
600 ml (1 pt) milk
300 ml (½ pt) water

1   Mix the rice with the coconut, chillies, salt, sugar, raisins, pistachios, bay leaves, cinnamon and cardamom pods.
2   Heat the ghee in a large saucepan over medium heat. Add the rice mixture and sauté for 5 minutes, stirring constantly.
3   Add the milk and water, increase the heat to high and bring to the boil. Stir.
4   Lower the heat to very low, cover and cook for about 20 minutes until all the liquid has evaporated. Fluff the pillau with a fork and serve hot.

Mushroom Pillau
(Khumbi Pillau)

Serves 4–6

2 tbsp oil
2 bay leaves
5 cm (2 in) cinnamon stick
4 green cardamom pods
1 large onion, finely chopped
175 g (6 oz) mushrooms, sliced
350 g (12 oz) basmati rice, washed and drained
1 tsp salt
900 ml (1½ pt) water

1 Heat the oil in a large saucepan over medium high heat. Add the bay leaves, cinnamon and cardamom pods and let them sizzle for a few seconds.
2 Add the onion and fry until soft. Add the mushrooms and fry for about 5 minutes until all the moisture has been absorbed.
3 Add the rice and salt and stir-fry for 2–3 minutes. Add the water and bring to the boil.
4 Cover tightly, lower the heat to very low and cook for about 20 minutes until all the water has been absorbed. Fluff the pillau with a fork and serve hot.

SNACKS AND SALADS

These snack recipes are extremely versatile. They are ideal for picnics as they can be eaten cold, served with a salad or chutney. They can form part of a meal as a side dish with a main course, or alternatively, as an hors d'oeuvre.

Spicy Pounded Rice
(Batata Poha)

Serves 4
100 g (4 oz) cooked, pounded rice
2 tbsp oil
½ tsp mustard seeds
1–2 dried red chillies, broken in half
1–2 green chillies, chopped
5–6 curry leaves
1 small onion, finely chopped
2 medium potatoes, boiled and diced
    into 1 cm (½ in) cubes
¼ tsp ground turmeric
1 tsp salt
½ tsp chilli powder
2 tsp lime juice
2 tbsp coriander leaves, chopped

1 Wash the pounded rice and leave to drain in a sieve for about 15 minutes.
2 Heat the oil over a medium high heat and add the mustard seeds; as soon as they start to splutter add the red chillies, green chillies and curry leaves and let them sizzle for 7–8 seconds.
3 Add the onion and stir-fry until golden.
4 Add the potatoes, turmeric, salt and chilli powder and mix with the onions.
5 Add the drained pounded rice and mix with the other ingredients; stir-fry for 2–3 minutes.
6 Lower the heat, cover and cook for about 8–10 minutes, stirring occasionally (add a little extra oil if you think it necessary).
7 Sprinkle on the lime juice and coriander leaves. Mix well and serve immediately. This is eaten for breakfast or as a light snack.

Savoury Puffed Rice
(Bhel Poori)

Serves 4–6
700 g (1½ lb) puffed rice
1 medium potato, boiled and diced
    into 5 mm (¼ in) cubes
1 small onion, finely chopped
2 tbsp coriander leaves, chopped
½ tsp salt

Tamarind chutney
about 120 ml (4 fl oz)
    thick tamarind juice
½ tsp salt
½ tsp chilli powder
½ tsp sugar

Green chutney
4 sprigs of coriander, washed
2 green chillies
½ tsp salt
2–3 tbsp lemon juice
a little water

1 Mix together the puffed rice, potato, onion, coriander leaves and salt and put aside.
2 Make the tamarind chutney by mixing together the tamarind juice, salt, chilli powder and sugar; put aside.
3 Make the green chutney by first chopping the coriander leaves and throwing away the lower stalks and roots.
4 Blend together the coriander leaves, green chillies, salt and lemon juice until smooth. Add a little water if necessary. This sauce should not be too thick.
5 When you are ready to serve the bhel poori, add the chutneys to the puffed rice mixture (the amount can vary to suit individual taste). Serve immediately as a snack.

Rice with Gram Flour Dumplings
(Gatte Ki Khichiri)

Serves 4

75 g (3 oz) gram flour	**Rice**
¼ tsp chilli powder	275 g (10 oz)
½ tsp ground	basmati rice
coriander	2 tbsp ghee
pinch of turmeric	1 tsp cumin seeds
½ tsp salt	½ tsp chilli powder
2 tbsp hot ghee	900 ml (1½ pt)
(see page 16)	boiling water
about 4 tbsp hot water	

1 Sieve the gram flour into a large bowl.
2 Mix in the chilli powder, coriander, turmeric and half the salt. Rub in the ghee.
3 Add enough water to make a firm dough and knead for 2–3 minutes.
4 Divide into 4 parts. Roll each ball into round strips 15 cm (6 in) long.
5 Bring some water to the boil and place these strips carefully in the water. Boil for 5 minutes. Drain and cool, then cut into 1 cm (½ in) pieces.
6 Wash the basmati rice in several changes of water. Leave the rice to soak for 20 minutes in plenty of water then drain.
7 In a large saucepan, heat the ghee over a medium high heat. Add the cumin seeds and let them sizzle for 3–4 seconds.
8 Add the rice, chilli powder and remaining salt, and sauté for 2–3 minutes.
9 Add the gram flour pieces carefully and gently mix with the rice. Fry for 1 minute.
10 Add the water and, when it starts to boil rapidly, lower the heat to very low, cover and cook for about 20 minutes until the rice is tender.
11 Fluff with a fork and serve hot.

Curry with Gram Flour Dumplings
(Gatte Ki Saag)

Serves 4

Dough

75 g (3 oz)
  gram flour
¼ tsp chilli powder
½ tsp ground coriander
good pinch of turmeric
¾ tsp salt
2 tbsp ghee
  (see page 16)
about 4 tbsp water

Curry

2 tbsp ghee
  (see page 16)
½ tsp cumin seeds
¼ tsp mustard seeds
pinch of asafoetida
120 ml (4 fl oz) yoghurt,
  beaten well
½ tsp chilli powder
3 tsp ground coriander
½ tsp ground turmeric
1 tsp salt
pinch of asafoetida

1. To make the dough, place the gram flour, chilli powder, coriander, turmeric and salt in a bowl. Rub in the ghee.
2. Add enough water to make a firm dough. Knead for 2–3 minutes.
3. Divide into 4 parts. Roll each ball between your palms into round strips 15 cm (6 in) long.
4. Bring some water to the boil, and place the strips into the water carefully. Boil for 5 minutes. Drain and cool. Cut into 1 cm (1½ in) pieces.
5. To make the curry, heat the ghee in a saucepan over a medium heat. Add the cumin seeds, mustard and asafoetida and let them splutter for 5–6 seconds.
6. Remove from the heat and add the yoghurt and the rest of the spices.
7. Stirring constantly, return the saucepan to the heat and cook for about 3–4 minutes (if you do not stir constantly the yoghurt might separate).
8. Add the gram flour pieces, mix gently with the gravy and cook for a further 5 minutes.

Fried Lentil Cakes
(Vada)

Serves 4

225 g (8 oz) channa
  dal, washed
1–2 green chillies,
  chopped
1 small onion, finely
  chopped

pinch of asafoetida
½ tsp chilli powder
  (optional)
½ tsp salt
oil for deep frying

1. Soak the dal in plenty of cold water for 4–5 hours. Drain.
2. Grind the dal coarsely in a food processor or blender. (If using a blender, add a little water only if necessary.)
3. Add the green chillies, onion, asafoetida, chilli powder and salt to the ground dal and mix well.
4. Heat the oil over a medium high heat.
5. Take a tbsp of the mixture in the palm of your hand, flatten it slightly and deep fry for 1–2 minutes until golden brown. Make all the lentil cakes in this way. Serve hot.

Spicy Lamb Wrapped with Potatoes
(Chop)

Serves 4

Filling

2 tbsp oil

1 large onion,
   finely sliced

2 cloves garlic,
   crushed

1 cm (½ in)
   ginger, grated

¾ tsp ground turmeric

½ tsp chilli powder

1 tsp salt

good pinch of sugar

1 tbsp raisins (optional)

2 tsp vinegar

450 g (1 lb) minced
   lamb

1 tsp ground garam
   masala

1 egg (slightly beaten)
breadcrumbs
oil for shallow frying

Chop

750 g (1¾ lb) potatoes,
   peeled and boiled

1 tsp ground
   roast cumin

½ tsp ground, roast,
   dried red chillies
   (optional)

1 tsp salt

1 To make the filling, heat the oil in a large frying pan over a medium high heat. Add the onion, garlic and ginger and fry for 4–5 minutes, stirring constantly, until the onion becomes pale gold.

2 Add the turmeric, chilli, salt, sugar, raisins and vinegar, mix thoroughly with the onion and fry for 1 minute. Add the lamb and mix with the spices.

3 Cover, lower the heat, and, stirring occasionally, cook for about 20 minutes. Remove the cover, turn the heat up and, stirring constantly, cook until all the liquid has evaporated and the lamb is dry.

4 Mix in the garam masala, remove from the heat and set aside to cool.

5 To make the chop, mash the potatoes with the cumin, chilli and salt. Divide into 20–22 balls.

6 Take a ball and make a depression in the middle with your thumb, to form a cup shape. Fill the centre with the meat and re-form the potato ball, making sure no cracks appear. Make all the chop in this manner. (The chop can be round and flat or long in shape.)

7 Place the chop in the beaten egg, one at a time, and roll in the breadcrumbs.

8 Heat the oil over a very high heat in a large frying pan and fry the chop until golden brown, turning once (about 1 minute).

Fried Potatoes
(Aloo Bhaja)

Serves 2
3–4 medium potatoes, peeled
½ tsp salt
oil for shallow frying

1 Slice the potatoes thinly and rub in the salt.
2 Heat the oil over a high heat and fry the potatoes until golden.

Fried Fish
(Mach Bhaja)

Serves 2
1 tsp salt
½ tsp ground turmeric
450 g (1 lb) medium-sized herring, cleaned
    and washed
oil for shallow frying

1 Rub the salt and turmeric into the fish and set aside for 15–20 minutes.
2 Heat the oil over a medium high heat and fry the fish for about 3–4 minutes on each side.

Fried Potato Cakes
(Aloo Tikka)

Serves 4
450 g (1 lb) potatoes, boiled and mashed
1–2 green chillies, chopped
½ tsp salt
1 tbsp coriander leaves, chopped
2 tbsp onions, chopped
oil for frying

1 Mix the mashed potatoes with the chillies, salt, coriander leaves and onions.
2 Form into small balls and flatten.
3 Heat the oil until hot and fry the potato cakes for a few minutes each side until golden. Serve with a chutney.

Fried Lentil Patties
(Dal Vada)

Serves 4
225 g (8 oz) urid dal, washed
5–6 curry leaves
2–3 green chillies
pinch of asafoetida
1 cm (½ in) ginger, grated
¾ tsp cumin seeds
½ tsp salt
oil for deep frying

1 Soak the urid dal in plenty of cold water overnight. Drain.
2 In a liquidiser or food processor, blend the dal with all the other ingredients. Add a little water, if necessary, to make a fine, thick paste.
3 Heat the oil over a medium high heat. Drop in a teaspoonful of the mixture and fry until nicely golden. Serve with a chutney as a snack or as an accompaniment to a main meal.

Samosas

Serves 4

Filling

3 tbsp oil

¼ tsp whole cumin seeds

450 g (1 lb) potatoes, diced into
    1 cm (½ in) cubes

1 green chilli, finely chopped

pinch of turmeric

½ tsp salt

75 g (3 oz) peas

1 tsp ground roast cumin (see page 18)

Dough

225 g (8 oz) plain flour

1 tsp salt

3 tbsp oil

about 100 ml (3½ fl oz) hot water

oil for deep frying

1 To make the filling, heat the oil in a large saucepan over medium high heat and add the cumin seeds. Let them sizzle for a few seconds.

2 Add the potatoes and green chilli and fry for 2–3 minutes. Add the turmeric and salt and, stirring occasionally, cook for 5 minutes.

3 Add the peas and the ground roast cumin. Stir to mix. Cover, lower the heat and cook a further 10 minutes until the potatoes are tender. Cool.

4 To make the dough, sieve together the flour and salt. Rub in the oil. Add enough water to form a stiff dough. Knead for 10 minutes until smooth.

5 Follow steps 1-7 on the opposite page to prepare and fill the samosas.

6 Heat the oil in a karai over medium heat. Put as many samosas as you can into the hot oil and fry until crisp and golden. Drain. Serve with a chutney.

Preparing the dough and filling the cones

1

Divide the dough into 12 balls.

2

Roll each ball into a round of about 15 cm (6 in) across.

3

Cut round in half.

4

Pick up one half, flatten it slightly and form a cone, sealing the overlapping edge with a little water.

5

Fill the cone with 1½ tsp of the filling.

6

Seal the top of the cone with a little water.

7

Make all the samosas in the same way.

Yoghurt Curry With Pakoras
(Karhi)

Serves 2
Pakoras

75 g (3 oz) gram flour	1 tbsp gram flour
¼ tsp salt	1 tbsp oil
pinch of ground turmeric	¼ tsp fenugreek seeds
	pinch of asafoetida
about 4 tbsp water	6–8 curry leaves
oil for deep frying	2 green chillies, chopped

Curry

	½ tsp ground turmeric
300 ml (½ pt) yoghurt	½ tsp chilli powder
350 ml (12 fl oz) water	½ tsp salt

1 To make the pakoras, make a thick batter with the gram flour, salt, turmeric and water.
2 Heat the oil over a medium high heat, drop in a teaspoonful of the batter and fry until crisp and golden. Drain and set aside.
3 To make the curry, whisk the yoghurt, water and gram flour until smooth.
4 Place the fried pakoras in a bowl of water for 3–4 minutes. Gently squeeze out as much water as possible and put aside.
5 Heat 1 tbsp oil in a large saucepan over a medium heat. Add the fenugreek, asafoetida, curry leaves and green chillies and let them sizzle for about 10 seconds.
6 Add the yoghurt mixture, turmeric, chilli and salt and slowly bring to the boil.
7 Lower the heat, add the pakoras and simmer for about 10 minutes until the sauce has thickened. Serve hot with rice.

Cucumber Salad
(Khamang Kakadi)

Serves 4
2 tbsp unsalted peanuts
½ cucumber, peeled and cut into fine strips
2 tbsp grated coconut
2 tbsp lemon juice
½ tsp salt
1 tbsp ghee (see page 16)
¼ tsp cumin seeds
pinch of asafoetida
2 green chillies, chopped
1 tbsp coriander leaves, chopped

1 Dry roast the peanuts and grind them to a fine powder.
2 Gently squeeze the cucumber to get rid of the excess water.
3 Place the cucumber, coconut, ground peanuts, lemon juice and salt in a bowl and mix gently.
4 In a small saucepan, heat the ghee. Add the cumin seeds and let them sizzle for 3–4 seconds. Add the asafoetida and the green chillies and fry for 5–6 seconds. Pour this over the cucumber mixture and mix well.
5 Garnish with the coriander leaves.

Cabbage Salad
(Kacha Pakka Kobi)

Serves 4
450 g (1 lb) green cabbage
1 tsp oil
2 green chillies, chopped
2 tsp urid dal
½ tsp mustard seeds
pinch of asafoetida
¾ tsp coconut, grated
1 tbsp coriander leaves, chopped

1 Cut the cabbage very finely into long strips. Wash and dry them.
2 Heat the oil in a large saucepan over a medium high heat. Add the chillies and fry for 3–4 seconds.
3 Remove the saucepan from the heat, add the urid dal and stir-fry until lightly golden (this will take a few seconds only).
4 Put the saucepan back on the heat and add the mustard seeds; after 8–10 seconds add the asafoetida and fry for 2–3 seconds.
5 Add the cabbage and salt and, stirring constantly, cook for 3–4 minutes. Serve garnished with the coconut and coriander leaves.

Spicy Sago
(Saboodana Ki Khichiri)

Serves 4

175 g (6 oz) sago
75 g (3 oz) peanuts, skinned
2 tbsp oil
1 tsp mustard seeds
2 green chillies, chopped
pinch of asafoetida
good pinch of turmeric
1 tsp salt
1 tsp sugar
about 5 tbsp water
juice of ½ a lime
1 tbsp coconut, grated
1 tbsp coriander leaves, chopped

1 Wash the sago and soak in a little water for about 10 minutes. Drain and dry on kitchen paper.
2 Roast the peanuts and grind coarsely.
3 Mix the sago and peanuts.
4 Heat the oil in a saucepan over a medium high heat. Add the mustard seeds and green chillies; when the mustard seeds start to splutter, add the asafoetida and fry for 2–3 seconds.
5 Add the sago and peanut mixture, turmeric, salt and sugar and stir-fry for 1 minute.
6 Lower the heat and continue to stir-fry for another 2–3 minutes.
7 Add the water, cover and cook, stirring occasionally, until the sago is tender and nearly dry.
8 Add the lime juice and give it a good stir. Serve garnished with coconut and coriander leaves.

Melon with Orange Juice
(Tarbuch Aur Mosamki Ka Rus)

Serves 4
1 honeydew melon
15 g (½ oz) butter or ghee
½ tsp ground cumin
juice of 2 sweet oranges
1 tbsp lemon juice
2 tbsp sugar

1 Cut the melon into segments, remove the pith and seeds and cut the flesh from the skin. Cut into cubes.
2 Heat the butter or ghee in a pan, add the cumin and let it sizzle until the fragrance emerges.
3 Meanwhile, mix the orange and lemon juice with the sugar and 1 tbsp water.
4 Sprinkle the syrup on the melon, add the cumin and serve.

Tomato Salad
(Kachumbar)

Serves 4
450 g (1 lb) tomatoes, sliced
2 green chillies, finely sliced
2 tsp sugar
1 tbsp lemon juice
leaves from 1 or 2 sprigs of coriander
salt

1 Mix the tomato with the chilli.
2 Sprinkle with sugar, lemon juice and coriander leaves. Mix well and add salt to taste.

Chicken and Vegetable Salad
(Murghi Aur Kachumbar)

Serves 4–6

225 g (8 oz) cooked chicken, cut into
   bite-sized pieces
1 or 2 apples, cored and cut into segments
75 g (3 oz) white cabbage, grated
2 tomatoes, cut into 8 pieces
1 green chilli, finely chopped
½ tsp ground black pepper
¼ tsp ground nutmeg
salt
2 tbsp lemon juice
1 or 2 sprigs of coriander

1 Mix the chicken with the apple, cabbage, tomato and green chilli.
2 Sprinkle on the pepper, nutmeg and salt.
3 Squeeze over the lemon juice and toss the salad. Garnish with coriander leaves.

Cabbage Fritters
(Gobi Pakoras)

Serves 4

100 g (4 oz) gram flour
100 g (4 oz) hard white cabbage, grated
1 small onion, finely sliced
2 green chillies, thinly sliced
5 g (½ oz) fresh ginger, finely grated
4–6 curry leaves, chopped
1 tsp salt
½ tsp chilli powder
½ tsp garam masala (see page 17)
oil for deep frying

1 Mix the flour with 150 ml (¼ pt) water to make a batter.
2 Add all the ingredients except the oil and stir well to coat.
3 Heat a quantity of oil for deep frying, add the cabbage in batter by the tablespoonful and fry until golden. Drain on absorbent kitchen paper.
4 Serve with chutney.

Mint Chutney
(Poodina Ki Chutney)

handful mint leaves, washed
50 ml (2 fl oz) tamarind juice
2 tbsp chopped onions
2 cloves garlic
2 cm (¾ in) ginger
2–3 green chillies
½ tsp salt
½ tsp sugar

1 Blend all the ingredients together until you have a smooth paste.

Chutney can be stored in an airtight container in the fridge for one week only.

Green Mango Relish
(Aam Chutney)

225 g (8 oz) hard green mango
50 g (2 oz) finely grated coconut
red chilli or 1 tsp chilli powder
1 tsp mustard seeds
1 tbsp yoghurt
1 tbsp oil
4 curry leaves
salt

1 Chop the mango as finely as possible, with or without the skin.

2 Grind, pound or blend in a liquidiser the coconut, chilli and half the mustard seeds, add to the mango and stir in the yoghurt.

3 Heat the oil in a pan, add the remaining mustard seeds and the curry leaves and fry until all the seeds have popped, then stir into the relish. Add salt to taste.

Black Lentil Curry
(Urid Dal Chutney)

75–100 g (3–4 oz) polished split black lentils (urid dal)
1 or 2 red chillies
1 tsp asafoetida
50 g (2 oz) finely grated coconut
juice from 25 g (1 oz) seedless tamarind (see page 16)
salt

1 Pick over the dal. Heat a saucepan without fat or oil, add the dal, 1 chilli and the asafoetida and cook, shaking the saucepan to prevent burning, until the dal is golden.

2 Pound the roast spices together.

3 Grind, pound or blend in a liquidiser the coconut and tamarind with 1–2 tbsp water, then add the roast spice powder and grind them together, adding a little more water if necessary.

4 Add salt to taste.

PUDDINGS

India offers a large variety of puddings and sweets. Indian desserts are often the climax of a meal and are much anticipated by diners. Most sweets are milk-based and can be prepared in advance.

Ice Cream with Almonds and Pistachio Nuts
(Kulfi)

Serves 6

1.2 litres (2 pt) milk
50 g (2 oz) sugar
2 tbsp ground almonds
2 tbsp pistachio nuts, skinned and chopped
few drops rosewater

1 Bring the milk to the boil, stirring constantly.
2 Lower the heat and simmer, stirring occasionally, until it reduces to about 500 ml (18 fl oz).
3 Add the sugar and mix thoroughly. Continue to simmer for another 2–3 minutes. Remove from the heat and let it cool completely.
4 Add the almonds and mix into the thickened milk, making sure no lumps form.
5 Stir in the pistachio nuts and rosewater.
6 Place the mixture in a dish, cover it with its own lid or aluminium foil and place it in the freezer.
7 Take it out of the freezer after 20 minutes and give it a good stir to break up the ice crystals. Repeat twice more.
8 After this, it may be divided up into six chilled single dishes, and covered and frozen for about 4–5 hours. Take it out of the freezer about 10 minutes before you are ready to serve. An alternative serving suggestion would be to prepare the ice cream as individual lollies, as seen below.

Gujarati-style Creamed Rice (Doodh Pak)

Serves 4
1.2 litres (2 pt) milk
25 g (1 oz) rice
40 g (1½ oz) sugar
½ tsp ground cardamom
1 tbsp ground almonds

1 Bring the milk to the boil, stirring constantly.
2 Add the rice and sugar; stir to mix. Lower the heat, and, stirring occasionally, simmer until the milk has thickened and is reduced to about 500 ml (18 fl oz).
3 Remove from the heat and stir in the cardamom and almonds, making sure no lumps form when the nuts are added. Serve with hot Poori (see page 112).

Baked Yoghurt (Payodhi)

Serves 4
410 g (14¼ oz) tin evaporated milk
397 g (14 oz) tin condensed milk
500 ml (18 fl oz) yoghurt
1 tbsp pistachio nuts, skinned and chopped
handful of almonds, to decorate

1 Preheat the oven to 225°C/450°F/Gas Mark 5.
2 Whisk the evaporated milk, condensed milk and yoghurt together for 1 minute.
3 Pour into an ovenproof dish and place in the preheated oven.
4 Turn the oven off after 6 minutes and leave the dish in the oven overnight.
5 Chill. Serve decorated with the chopped pistachio nuts and almonds (see picture below).

Gram Flour Balls
(Besan Laddu)

Serves 4
175 g (6 oz) gram (chickpea) flour
6 tbsp ghee (see page 16)
100 g (4 oz) sugar
1 tbsp chopped pistachios

1   Sieve the gram flour.
2   Heat the ghee in a heavy-based saucepan over a medium heat and fry the gram flour until golden.
3   Remove from the heat and cool. Add sugar and mix well.
4   When cold, make into small balls about the size of a walnut. Roll each ball in the chopped pistachios.

Yoghurt with Saffron
(Shrikhand)

Serves 4

600 ml (1 pt) yoghurt
¼ tsp saffron
1 tbsp warm milk
100 g (4 oz) caster sugar
2 tbsp pistachio nuts, skinned and chopped

1 Put the yoghurt in a muslin bag and hang it up for 4–5 hours to get rid of the excess water.
2 Soak the saffron in the milk for 30 minutes.
3 Whisk together the drained yoghurt, sugar and saffron milk until smooth and creamy.
4 Put in a dish and garnish with the nuts. Chill until set.

Fritters in Syrup
(Malpoa)

Serves 4

200 g (7 oz) plain flour
1½ tsp baking powder
175 ml (6 fl oz) yoghurt
about 175 ml (6 fl oz) milk
225 g (8 oz) sugar
450 ml (16 fl oz) water
oil for deep frying

1 Sieve together the flour and baking powder. Mix in the yoghurt. Add enough milk to make a thick batter.
2 Boil the sugar and water together for 10 minutes.
3 Heat the oil in a karai over medium high heat. Drop in 1 tbsp of the batter at a time and fry until crisp and brown. Drain on kitchen paper.
4 Soak the fried malpoa in the syrup for 5 minutes. Serve in a little syrup, hot or cold.

Saffron Rice
(Zaffrani Chawal)

Serves 4–6

275 g (10 oz) basmati rice
½ tsp saffron
about 1 litre (1¾ pt) boiling water
5 tbsp ghee (see page 16)
2–3 cardamom pods
50 g (2 oz) almonds, slivered
65 g (2½ oz) sugar
1 tbsp pistachio nuts, chopped

1 Wash the rice and soak in water for 15 minutes. Drain thoroughly. Soak the saffron in 2 tbsp of the boiling water for 15 minutes.
2 Heat the ghee in a large saucepan over a medium high heat; add the cardamom pods and sizzle for 3–4 seconds. Add the rice and almonds and, stirring constantly, fry until lightly golden.
3 Add the boiling water, saffron and sugar and stir. Turn the heat down low, cover and cook for about 20 minutes until all the water has been absorbed and the rice is tender. Fluff with a fork, garnish with pistachio nuts and serve.

Cheese Balls in Syrup
(Rassogolla)

Serves 4
300 g (11 oz) paneer (see page 15), drained
175 g (6 oz) ricotta cheese
350 g (12 oz) sugar
1.25 l (2¼ pt) water

1 Rub the paneer and ricotta cheese with the palms of your hands until smooth and creamy. Divide into 16 balls.

2 Boil the sugar and water for 5 minutes over medium heat. Put the balls in the syrup and boil for 40 minutes.

3 Cover and continue to boil for another 30 minutes. Serve warm or cold.

GLOSSARY

Adrak Fresh ginger (see below).

Amchur Dried mango powder. Has a bittersweet flavour.

Asafoetida A truffle-flavoured brown resin, available in powdered or lump form, and often used in cooking with beans. If you buy the lump form, crumble off a small piece and crush it between two sheets of paper.

Basmati rice The finest Indian long-grained rice, grown in the foothills of the Himalayas.

Besan Also known as gram flour, this is the flour made from chickpeas. It is used particularly in the south for making pancakes and steamed patties.

Biriyani A rice and vegetable, meat or seafood oven-cooked dish.

Boondi Small deep-fried balls made out of gram flour.

Cardamom Both black and green cardamoms are available, although the black ones are not often available. They are large and hairy. Use the green ones for the recipes in this book.

Channa dal A very versatile dried split pea. It looks like the ordinary yellow split pea, but is smaller with a sweeter, nuttier flavour. It can be cooked until soft for the dish called simply "dal", or, as in southern India, it can be used as a spice.

Chawal Rice.

Chickpeas Also called gram or, in America, garbanzo beans. Because chickpeas often demand hours of cooking before they become tender, it is often cheaper to buy the tinned variety unless you have an old-fashioned kitchen range.

Chillies Can be bought fresh, in which case they are normally green, or dried, in which case they are red. Chillies are very hot and should be handled with care and used according to taste.

Cinnamon Can be bought powdered, or, better, in sticks. These sticks are the rolled bark of the cinnamon tree and have a warm spicy flavour.

Coconut Characteristic of the cooking of southern India. Buy a fresh coconut to extract the milk (see page 18) or use desiccated coconut to thicken sauces or garnish finished dishes. Desiccated coconut can be bought in most supermarkets and delicatessens.

Coriander Both the seeds and leaves of this plant are used. It can be grown as easily as parsley. The seeds are small and round and are used either whole or ground. The leaves are bright green and have a strong bittersweet flavour.

Cumin seeds White or black, these seeds can be used whole or ground.

Curry leaves Can sometimes be bought fresh, which is preferable to using them dried. Used extensively in the south of India, they are mainly added to food just before it is ready.

Dahi Yoghurt.

Dalchini Cinnamon (see above).

Dals Dried split peas, usually bought skinned.

Dhaniya Coriander (see above).

Elaichi Cardamom (see above).

Fenugreek seeds Chunky, tawny-coloured seeds, often used roasted and ground. They have a bitter taste. Fenugreek leaves are a vegetable used like spinach, to which the plant is related.

Garam masala A mixture of spices ground together (see page 17), it is sprinkled on some dishes after they have been cooked.

Ghee Drawn butter. It can be made at home (see page 16) and does not need to be refrigerated.

Ginger Fresh ginger (adrak) is a fawn-coloured rhizome. Ginger can also be bought powdered (soondth).

Gosht Meat. Goat is the meat most often eaten in India.

Gram flour Made from chickpeas and also known as besan.

Haldi Turmeric (see below).

Halva A sweet dish.

Hing Asafoetida (see above).

Imli Tamarind (see below).

Jaggery Raw sugar, eaten as it is and used to flavour various dishes, even vegetable curries.

Jeera Cumin (see above).

Jingha Prawn.

Kofta Meat or banana balls.

Kumban Mushroom.

Lassi A yoghurt drink (see page 16).

Luong Cloves.

Machi Fish.

Masala Spices.

Masoor dal Skinned split red lentils.

Moong dal Skinned split mung beans.

Murghi Chicken.

Mustard oil A yellow oil made from mustard seeds that is pungent when raw and sweet when heated. Much used in Kashmir and Bengal.

Mustard seeds Small yellow or black seeds often popped in hot oil, when they have a nutty sweet flavour. When ground for mustard powder their character is quite different – hot and smarting.

Nigella seeds Tiny triangular-shaped black seeds known as kalonji in India and used in cooking. They are commonly seen studded on some Indian breads.

Narial Coconut (see above).

Neem Curry leaves (see above).

Panch phoron Also known as Bengali five-spice, this is a mixture of five spices. The five spices are, fenugreek, nigella seeds, cumin seeds, black mustard seeds and fennel seeds in equal parts.

Papaya A fruit with good digestive properties.

Pilau Fried rice dish.

Raita A cooling side dish made with yoghurt.

Roti Bread.

Sago Edible starch that is extracted from the sago palm. It is dried to produce a flour or processed into a granular form.

Sambar powder A southern Indian spice mix for vegetable curries (see page 11).

Soondth Powdered ginger (see above).

Tamarind The bean-like fruit of the tamarind tree, much used in southern Indian cooking.

Tava A flat cast-iron pan used for making bread.

Thali A large tray, often of wrought metal.

Toran A style of cooking where the dish remains dry.

Toovar dal A glossy dark yellow split pea.

Urid dal Polished split black lentils, often used as a spice in southern India.

Vark Silver and golf leaf used to decorate food on special occasions. It is edible.

Vindaloo A highly spiced and hot curry, traditionally from Goa.

Index

Acknowledgements

The publishers would like to thank the following picture libraries for their kind permission to use their pictures:

Istock: 18, 23, 38, 69, 76, 77, 119, 151

Shutterstock: 8, 9, 10, 11, 16, 17, 21, 25, 29, 31, 35, 37, 41, 42, 46, 49, 51, 54, 56, 61, 62, 64, 66. 68, 71, 75, 78, 79, 80, 82, 85, 89, 90, 92, 98, 99, 100, 101, 103, 104, 105, 106, 114, 115, 118, 122, 134, 125, 131, 132, 135, 137, 139, 143, 145, 147, 150, 153, 154, 156, 158, 159, 163, 164, 167, 169

Photocuisine: 45, 96

Stockfood: front cover

Every effort has been made to contact the copyright holders for images reproduced in this book. The Publisher would welcome any errors or omissions being brought to their attention and apologizes in advance for any unintentional omissions or errors. The Publisher will be pleased to insert the appropriate acknowledgement to any companies or individuals in any subsequent edition of the work.